A TEACHER'S QUEST 2.0

Serving Students and Saving the Schools

BRIAN L. MURPHY

PRIMIX
PUBLISHING
THE WRITE CHOICE

Primix Publishing
11620 Wilshire Blvd
Suite 900, West Wilshire Center, Los Angeles, CA, 90025
www.primixpublishing.com
Phone: 1-800-538-5788

Published by Primix Publishing: 05/30/2025

ISBN: 979-8-89194-168-7(sc)
ISBN: 979-8-89194-169-4(e)

Library of Congress Control Number: 2024907625

CONTENTS

CHAPTER 1

Q: How did I Get Here?

A: I chose to be here.

I N OCTOBER OF 1997, I received a phone call that would quickly change my career path and my life.

In May of 1970, I graduated from Washington High School in Fremont, California, along with many thousands of 1960 vintage wannabe hippies, who graduated that year, far too many of whom wanted to save the planet and the future by becoming teachers. Unfortunately, the law of supply and demand was still functioning, and this glut of prospective applicants and a shortage of positions available led to a salary range that was at best pitiful, even if you could land a job. Still in college,

I decided to change my major to the biggest umbrella field I could think of—Business Administration with a focus on Management. In May of 1976, I received my bachelor's degree in business and embarked on a career in manufacturing management that began as a "worker bee/ individual contributor," then evolved to a supervisor position, and then to a management position over the course of eighteen years. The variety of products I worked on ranged from medical diagnostics (making kits that tested soldiers coming home from Vietnam for drug abuse) to agricultural chemicals (making ecologically sensitive weed killer for farmers across America) and then electronics. To make a long story as short as possible, the final company I worked for, the electronics company, was the second largest computer company in the world, second only to IBM, Digital Equipment Corporation (DEC). In the 1960s and '70s, DEC had made a fortune selling desktop computers (big enough to literally take up the top of an average sized desk), and they shunned the market opportunities of PCs and in-home computers. DEC upper management swore their assurances that "toy" computers were a fad and that no one was going to want a computer in their home. How wrong could they have been? In a few short years, DEC was bankrupted and gone from the market, leaving tens of thousands of employees laid off, including me.

Then I had a choice to make. I was good at what I did, maybe the best I had ever seen. (For everything that gets made in America or anywhere, it's someone's job to determine when and how many final items need to get made and to make sure that all the component parts have been made or purchased beforehand and are available to use. That's what I did.) I enjoyed the work. But did I want to do it for another twenty years? I was thirty-eight years old, married, and open to a change. This was when my wife asked me the mother of all career questions: "If you could do anything and money was no problem, what would you want to do?" Without missing a heartbeat, I replied, "I'd become a teacher." I went back to San Jose State University, spent nearly two years taking classes and more time substituting for other teachers, and by the fall of 1997, I had a freshly minted teacher's credential.

To step back a minute, besides all the classes required for my business degree, I had always loved taking history, sociology, economics, and especially psychology classes, to the point that during my original total of six years in college, I had taken almost all the social studies classes my schools had to offer. When it came time to have my scholastic competence signed off for my credential at San Jose State, besides my business classes, I showed the head of the Social Studies department my list of classes taken, and he signed off on my competence in his department as well. So my teaching credential listed both business and social studies.

On that morning in October of 1997, I was sitting at my kitchen table, drinking coffee and looking forward to spending the day playing my favorite video game, when I got the call. It was my student-teacher supervisor from San Jose State.

"Hey, Brian, how are you? Are you working?" I had finished my second year subbing at all levels for my local school district and truly loving it.

"Yeah, I'm subbing."

"Do you want a full-time job?" the familiar voice on the phone asked.

That was the moment. A devil on one shoulder was saying, "Your free days are a lot of fun. Do you really want to give them up for the hassles of a job?"

But on my other shoulder was the angel of my better nature, my Irish Catholic responsible side, saying, "Okay, you're nearly forty years old, and you've been playing for two years. It's time."

"Yes, of course," I said, still not sure.

He laughed.

He gave me the name and number of a contact at a high school I knew nothing about, except that they had a job opening that I was qualified for. I called, met with the people there, and got the job. After all this time training and preparing, I was really going to get paid to be a teacher, so now what? I had no idea what I had stepped into.

And even as well "qualified" as I was on paper, stepping into the unknown was scary and brought out all of my insecurities. What do you do with that many kids every day? What are the kids like? What do the kids know, and what do they need to learn? Can you expect help from the administration? What about parents?

I had heard exciting stories about the future of American education and an equal number of horrible stories about other people's first years on the job. And, of course, I had questions of my own. That was twenty years ago, and each of the teachers I have talked to since, not to mention the dozen or so student teachers I've mentored over the years, have had their own list of "things I wish I had known at the beginning." So with an eye toward giving new teachers insight into what they are getting into, I decided to help fill the void and write a book. I also want this book to be a personal chronicle of my walk through that world with an eye toward explaining what is really happening in our schools and identifying some of its most severe problems.

However, this book will not be an overly impersonal collection of theories, charts, graphs, and columns of statistics. There are shelves of books like that, and if we could address the most severe problems in education using them, we would have done so by now. And to use the word *severe* is not an overstatement. I also want to give new or prospective teachers, parents, or other members of the education community a guidebook through the wondrous world of teaching. And since "identifying problems without offering solutions is just whining" (Teddy Roosevelt), besides being highly critical, I've offered solutions, including my vision of how the educational system could be changed to fulfill the needs of not only students and their families but also teachers and other professionals.

Research for *A Teacher's Quest* began with my asking colleagues in my Northern California school district, "What's gone wrong around here? And what are one or two things which would have been helpful to have known at the beginning of your career?" Scores of both new teachers and veteran teachers were gracious enough to share, and I've incorporated their comments. The most common comment from the veterans was, not surprisingly, "I wish I had known how much work it was."

However, our customers are unsatisfied. After reading the newspapers and hearing official reports on the state of education in America, many taxpayers and people outside education believe that the public school system is not getting the job done, and they wonder why. Trying not to offend, they ask: "We know that teachers work hard and that they make personal sacrifices for our children, but what needs to be done to make the system work better?" State and local governments get into the argument, as do the teachers' unions, an array of nonprofit organizations, and even the Federal government. However, for me, this is personal. For twenty years, I have loved being a teacher. But my love is in trouble, even dying, and I desperately want to both identify the problems faced in classrooms today and begin a discussion about what we can do to address them. The truth is that the school system is not getting the job done. Students today are not being prepared for a useful future, and teachers are quitting the profession in droves, and still supporting education is not a high priority in America. The problems we face are severe, the stakes are high, and the threat to our collective future is all too real.

CHAPTER 2

Q: So What Is Wrong?

A: Society is losing faith in our product.

PROMINENT AMONG THE BASIC problems we face in schools and society today is the fact that students are losing their willingness to cooperate with, let alone value or even appreciate, the schools their parents, the taxpayers, spend billions of dollars to fund and in which they themselves are forced by law to invest years of their time. Many young people, though they have been told it's true time after time, are simply not convinced a connection exists between sitting in a classroom and a more favorable future. And they are right. In truth, the experience of high school, as constituted today, will not directly prepare them to do anything useful, except perhaps to endure more education in the form of some level of college. At the same time, most of today's high school graduates allow themselves to be ushered into some level of continued education because they know that if they don't get in trouble and if they stay in high school and then "go to college," their parents will feed them, house them, and will generally shield them from experiencing the stark realities connected with having a job that they see in their parents' everyday lives; at least, they can delay it a few more years.

And it's true, their parent's everyday life in the outside world of adults is getting more difficult, more expensive, and generally, harder. And perhaps, as a result, more and more parents have come to see being able to protect their child from anything unpleasant as their first duty as parents. This goal can bring them into direct conflict with the schools if the schools insist on holding students accountable in preparation for a future where adults are forced to perform to accepted norms and where there are consequences for failure.

Because parents' lives are getting harder and because they believe that doing so will make their personal lives easier as well as make things better for their children, parents today are increasingly willing to surrender what should be their most basic responsibility as parents: molding and developing their children's moral compass and setting the children's expectations as to what the world outside will expect of them. More and more parents have come to expect that developing these traits in their children should be the responsibility of the public education system, which they pay their taxes to support. Parents send their children, dressed with all manner of body parts exposed, then accuse the school of sexism if the child is sent home to change clothes (boys or girls). When a child is caught cheating on a paper or a test, the parents will accuse the teacher and the school of treating the child unfairly, even threatening lawsuits. As a result, schools have folded under public and political pressure to accept highly questionable behavior in the name of being inclusive, politically correct, and "non-judgmental." These fundamental conflicts, where the school is concerned with enforcing norms for the good of all children and where the parents' want no consequences to befall their child, for any reason, play a part in leaving all the participants, the parents, the students, the school staff, and society in general frustrated and dissatisfied.

Parents point to the schools and say, "Solve my kid's

problems," the students see very little reward for the time and effort asked of them, and the teachers have their dreams of educating children dashed on the rocks of the student's seeming indifference.

CHAPTER 3

Q: What Do People Go Through to Become Teachers?

A: It's an evolving struggle, but it goes on.

TO BE A TEACHER, a candidate must, of course, navigate grades 1 through 12, followed by four to six years spent earning a bachelor's degree, some volunteer time in classrooms to get into the teacher education program, and more years of graduate school to get a credential. In the old days, a candidate took ten post-graduate education classes, including phase one of student teaching (usually a few weeks in an established teacher's classroom for two classes, mostly observing) followed by phase two student teaching (observing for a week or two and then actually planning for and running the class under the watchful eyes of a mentor teacher for a full semester). Then after getting their "Preliminary Credential," the candidate could look for a job and take extra classes in Technology, Health, and Mainstreaming the Gifted Child to receive a much more valued "Cleared" credential. I do not use the term "master teacher" but prefer "mentor teacher" in referring to those experienced teachers who supervise student teachers. Contrary to the way some veteran teachers see them, student teachers are not slaves nor primarily a source of free labor to grade student work. I was fortunate in my mentor teachers, but now that I am one and often share a student teacher with another experienced teacher, I see that some current teachers who take on student teachers take pride in the term "master teacher" as an insignia of rank, and they see themselves as part of a filtering process, trying to help identify those student teachers who should not get their credential because they "won't make it as a teacher," as if they knew. In my experience, this "filtering" activity is usually done by existing teachers who have questionable classroom abilities of their own, more so questionable ethics. It takes no intelligence of any kind to crush the dream of an inexperienced person put under your tutelage. In that case, you're just a bully. If a student teacher does happen to get paired with one of these, they should do their best to get reassigned. It can be difficult, and student teaching supervisors may not want to go through the extra work involved in placing them again (and because relatively few teachers ask to be mentors, changing an unfortunate master teacher may not be possible.) However, the change may be necessary for the student teacher's ultimate preparation.

The only reason to become a mentor teacher is to help build up the new generation and to help them achieve what could be the first big success in their new career. Undoubtedly some may exist, but in the years that I've mentored a dozen or so of the next generation of educators, I've yet to find a single case where, after jumping through all the hoops the universities make young people jump through, and after paying the expenses and providing the free labor they are forced to, I could not find some way to help that future teacher succeed. If a person gets to the student teacher part of their training and has earned the right to give teaching a shot, we owe it to them to give them a big enough first win to sustain them for a while. As a mentor, it's our job to do everything we can to help make them a success. It's true, being a teacher is hard, and not everyone can survive the preparation for it, let alone have the mix of drive and patience to ply the trade. But our student teachers, those who decide to make the attempt, are as much the future of America as the students are, maybe more.

Another thing people in the student teaching preparation system need to keep in mind is that those young people who become student teachers are not children but adults with adult responsibilities, most of whom need to work in grocery stores, restaurants, or retail stores in order to survive. Generally bright, excited, and willing to learn, student teachers schedule their lives around being on campus, where, while continuing to attend night classes, they must pay the college they go to be sent to a school for two stints of student teaching, where, during each phase, they can work for months at a time for free. Fortunately, as I will discuss later, in this area, things are getting better. There has been, during the length of my career, a dire shortage of people willing to become teachers. Those young people who are willing to take the challenge should be, and happily now are, better supported.

When my generation of teachers came up after we took our classes and did two stints as a student teacher, the state Department of Teacher Credentialing awarded us a "Preliminary Teaching Credential," and we could go off and find a job (or as in my case, be a substitute and be lucky enough to get a call). But once hired, we were generally on our own. We got a job, a subject to teach, a key to a classroom, another key, and directions to the faculty restroom, and we were left alone to do our thing. Every teacher of that era I know has horror story(s) of their first year, of being thrown into the deep end of the pool of education and being made to prove that they could survive. For example, since my "call" was in October, that meant that my school had marched a succession of substitute teachers through that class from the beginning of school in August. The result was while I was trying to invent the how of teaching my subject on a day-to-day basis, I was also finding out what the students had done, figuring out what the next step for them was, learning the school procedures, and checking if there were textbooks. For the students to take me seriously, I had to prove to them that I was going to be there for them, at least that I was going to be the one giving them the grade and the units they needed to graduate and that it was okay to connect with me. I could tell them I was here to stay, but I'm sure that is what the others had said or, at least, had implied. Why should they believe? I think it was easier for me because I was an older guy, forty-two, and because it was a business class and I had actually been out in the business world. They sometimes listen to someone who has been there, someone who has stories.

Beginning in the fall of 1998, the state of California changed the process of becoming a teacher. From that date until January of 2018, in addition to the ten classes I had to take, teacher candidates have been required to pass the Performance Assessment of California Teachers (PACT), the submission to the state of a compilation of lesson plans, student work, and videos created during the candidates' phase two teaching stint, accompanied by reflections and commentary on what the candidate did in the unit and why they did it. PACT amounts to a roughly sixty-page portfolio, prompted by worksheets with sometimes vague questions for the teacher candidate to answer under the gun of twelve different rubrics, which, if they don't manage to figure out the question correctly and answer it with enough detail and thought, even after all the years they've spent in classrooms preparing, they can be denied their lowest level Credential.

Once the student teacher is notified that they have passed their PACT, and not every candidate does pass, they are awarded their preliminary credential. Now they, too, can look for and get a teaching job. However, there is more training to come. For the first two or more years of their career, to receive a "Cleared" credential, the new teachers were required to pass the Beginning Teacher Support and Assessment program (BTSA), a "state- funded, job embedded, formative assessment system of support and professional growth for clearing preliminary credentials." What happened was that the district, in conjunction with the State Office of Teacher Credentialing, hired experienced teachers to travel between campuses to meet with first-and second year teachers to support and help them keep their lesson plans well thought through and delivered. The new teachers were also required to meet in the evening or on weekends with other new teachers to exchange ideas and experiences. According to those who have finished the program, the value of BTSA is directly determined by which mentor is assigned to them. Reports range from "She was a lifesaver, the reason I am still a teacher" to "The BTSA crap was just another hoop I was made to jump through." In the long run, though adding to their work-load, it looks like the BTSA program did help to support new teachers.

To keep up the imagery of constant evolution, the latest

and greatest version of teacher support is called CALPS (Cognitive Academic Language Proficiency Skills). According to those going through this latest version, it's the old BTSA with more lesson planning, increased emphasis on written analysis, academic word usage, and additional filming of their in-class performances for group appraisal at their universities.

Once we have teachers selected and trained, how are they now, and how should they be evaluated in the future? That's a fair question. To say that teachers or any working group can be paid by the taxpayers and yet be allowed to do what they like and go unsupervised, no matter how well intentioned, is unacceptable, to say the least. The evaluation process (in my California school district, which is likely to be different than those in other states and locations) is clearly and specifically described in our union contract (as discussed in chapter 13).

Using a traditional evaluation model (as described in the contract), the school's administrators are the school's management, and contractually, it's their job to supervise and evaluate the people working there and make sure the school's goals are met. However, there are problems as to what is practical. In my school, there are 110 teachers, half of whom are scheduled to be evaluated each year, and a metre three administrators, each of whom has an ever-lengthening list of other immediate daily duties they must get done. According to the union contract, an official, very detailed process must be used to evaluate each teacher individually, and over the years, those details have made the process too procedurally difficult, time-consuming, and labor intensive for administrators to move beyond a minimal evaluation, let alone take the extra steps required to put non-effective teachers on any kind of corrective action and then monitor that process. In the end, most of the supervising administrators simply don't do an adequate job of it, resulting in "bad teachers" who "don't teach" being allowed to stay, getting paid more each year until they retire. And we all have memories of that teacher who never seemed to do anything and from whom we learned nothing.

As it is now, the evaluation process at my school district requires that every two years or so, the majority of teachers (those with less than ten years with the district) are labeled as "on track for evaluation," which means that sometime in the first semester, he/she will be notified that they will be evaluated. Then on an agreed-upon date, the teacher and whatever administrator is to do the evaluation sit together and agree on the type of evaluation it is to be: a traditional visit, where the students are working on group work, or some other common activity, where the evaluator can see if all students are participating and if the teacher is actively involved. If both of these things are occurring, the observer says so in his report, and the teacher is deemed to be doing an acceptable job. One problem with this process is that the incoming evaluator generally has no background in the subject being "taught," and since they know exactly what day and period of the day the evaluator is coming, most teachers have developed a special activity to have the children do that will show them all being actively involved and where the teacher can seem to be about the room actively helping them. I don't know if it's a true story, but I've heard of a teacher who, knowing which day and period the evaluator was coming, arranged with his students that during the class discussion planned for that day and for his evaluation, if the student wanted to answer the question, they were to vigorously raise their right hands and he would call on them. However, if they definitely did not want to be called on while the administrator was in the room, they should, with equal energy, raise their left hand, and he promised not to call on them. During the discussion being evaluated, what the evaluator saw was a room full of students with their hands up, actively participating in the discussion. And every child called on seemed to know the answer.

The alternative type of evaluation, the nontraditional version, has the teacher involved as a team member with other teachers working on a project that in some way is related to their classes. As for evaluating the nontraditional version, not only does the evaluator not have enough subject knowledge to adequately understand what they are seeing, but it can also be nearly impossible for the evaluator to separate the work done by only one member of a team when it comes to accomplishing a mutual goal.

According to the process detailed in my district's union contract, if the observation is deemed less than acceptable, when the teacher and the administrator meet again, the Administrator of Record must provide a list of improvements that are suggested to the teacher, and there is a second observation scheduled during the second semester. If the suggested improvements are not made, the teacher can be put on a Remedial track and then the Unacceptable track, including retraining and improvement deadlines, which, if not successful, can end with the teacher's termination.

So what should we do instead? The process used to evaluate a teacher's performance should answer the two questions asked by the newly installed teacher preparation system, the PACT: what does the teacher plan to do in the classroom over the long run? And what do they plan to do on a given day? If the administrator or whoever is delegated to do the evaluation (and some have said that it should be another experienced teacher, perhaps even from the same department) or a mixed group of each can turn the required pre- evaluation conference into a discussion of the teacher's process and long-term goals for the class, then the observation on the agreed-to date can have some context. (The contractual problem of having other teachers doing the evaluation is that this requires members of labor to perform management functions.)

No matter how much seniority a teacher has, being a teacher can be a solitary existence. Even though there are thousands of people on our campus, being a teacher means being alone with thirty or forty children at a time, for roughly an hour, five or even six times a day. But it can be a crushingly lonely experience. New teachers should never sit quietly insulated in their assigned room and let things buildup. On the contrary, all teachers should form a network of coworkers that they can share experiences with, a group that they can laugh with or grumble about the states of things with and go out socially with.

And no teacher or administrator needs sixteen-to-eighteen-year- old "friends," no matter how "mature" they seem. This is dynamite waiting to blow up in the face of everyone involved. There are rules people working with children must live by. One, never be alone in a room with a child, and if doing so is absolutely unavoidable, keep the door wide open. Two, never put your hands on a student for any reason. Three, never take something from a child. If you need to confiscate something, hold your hand out and insist the child hand it to you. If they refuse, get help from the office and have the office person remove the child or the offending item. Above all, if you are responsible for children and their actions, think through what you will do in a strenuous situation before you need to do it. Don't even allow the appearance of inappropriate behavior. These children can and will get the wrong idea of anything you say or do.

One time, in my own experience, I was lecturing a class of eleventh graders on the Dark Ages, the Enlightenment, and the Protestant Reformation. While speaking about the "Ninety-five Theses" posted on the door of his church by Martin Luthor, I mentioned that Martin Luthor was a Catholic monk. What was heard by one child and reported to the principal was that I had called Rev. Martin Luthor King Jr. a "monkey," a clear racial slur that I would never or never did say.

The fact is that even if a teacher does not do or say anything wrong, they can and are being accused. Children will look their teachers or their school principal (or any other authority figure) in the eye and lie through their teeth if it's in their interests or if they can avoid getting in trouble. People working in schools have worked hard and long to have their careers, and a single accusation, true or false, can immeasurably damage them.

Beyond forming a social network, whether a new teacher or a seasoned veteran, teachers and other school employees should strive to become a part of the school community, join committees and schoolwide work groups, and become known. In education, as in any organization, it's better to be known as a "team player," the one we can all expect to have our backs, the reliable one, a member of the tribe.

But this will not save a career if or when there are accusations.

Becoming a teacher is a long and difficult journey. And yet, after they receive their credentials, roughly half of new teachers leave the profession in their first five years (between 40 and 50 percent according to the Alliance for Excellent Education). Although steps are being taken in some districts, something in education—either the pressure, the vulnerability, the disrespect, or a combination of things—is dreadfully wrong and getting worse.

CHAPTER 4

Q: How Does One Decide What Grade
   to Teach?

A: Subbing—a great way to test the waters.

ONE OF THE MOST important choices a teacher candidate has to make, at least in California, is which one of two kinds of credential they want to get—a multiple subject credential (for elementary grades) or a single subject credential (for middle school and high schools); and future teachers should experiment with all levels in the school system in order to intelligently decide which one is best for them. Subbing is a great way to do this. For two years, I took jobs subbing at elementary schools in my small town at both middle schools and the single high school included in the district. I found that I truly loved being with grades 7 and 8. It's a wonderfully innocent world where the onslaught of raging puberty crashes against the required structure of organized civilization. Little girls of middle school age (eleven to thirteen) spend their time adorably prancing around like little ponies, giggling and hugging one another. The boys are just kind of lost at that age. They know there are requirements in life, and they do not want to appear foolish, but they do not know quite what they should do at any time. For me, being with them at that time in life was quite an education in itself. All of us boys felt lost at that age, but we all thought we were the only ones. If you spend time with them, you see that you are not the only one. Even the socially "cool" boys feel misplaced at that age, and maybe we weren't so ridiculous after all.

Subbing: the very first job I was sent out on was to fill in for a kindergarten teacher. Picture all six foot one, 250 pounds of me in a room full of wide eyed tiny children sitting in miniature furniture. Standing in the back of the room while the principal introduced me, one little blond-haired boy looked down at my size 12 feet and then slowly up my frame, up to my face, and wondrously exclaimed, "You're big." One thing I realized at that moment was that I had to see things from their viewpoint. I was the new element entering their "normal." That day, my first day as a substitute teacher, I gained a real appreciation for the women, and a very few men, who teach these little people on a day-to-day basis. Imagine being locked in a room with five-year-olds, six-year-olds, or seven-year-olds for hours at a time. And what these teachers do with these children is literally amazing.

Lower-grade teachers establish a rigorously followed schedule so that every child knows exactly what is going on and what is going to happen next. Loving by nature, these teachers work to make the children feel loved and personally appreciated. They also teach them a sense of order and responsibility. And the children respond, proud of themselves and the responsibilities they have.

A couple quick stories: on that same first assignment, it was just me and the children, and you have to remember that even though we have thirty eight nieces and nephews, my wife and I never had children of our own. So what did I know? The regular teacher had left a schedule that the children were used to, so when it was time for the Pledge of Allegiance, I said, "Okay, let's say our pledge." I stood and faced the flag, my hand over my heart, ready to lead them. The children all stood with me, but in a moment, I felt a tiny hand on my arm. Looking down, I saw a determined five-year-old, who told me, "Mr. Murphy, that's my job." And, of course, it was. I quickly stepped aside, and he carried on, standing strong and leading his class, proudly doing "his job." As that first day went on, I came to appreciate how easy it would be to love these kids.

I realized how completely out of place I was that day, though I was the only teacher in the room. I had learned as a supervisor and manager in the business world that "if you are in command, you have to command. If you are in charge, be in charge." But now the schedule said it was Story Time followed by Singing Time, and that was to be done from a large, puffy chair in one corner of the room. The kids took care of me, and soon I was seated in the large, puffy chair with a room full of tiny people surrounding me, sitting cross-legged on the rug covered floor with their hands in their laps and their backs very tall. This was their power position. They knew what book was to be read from and exactly where in the book they had left off, so continuing the reading was easy and fun. Since I had decided to myself that this day I would go for it and have fun, my reading was at times quite animated. The kids laughed and seemed to enjoy it. But Singing Time was a little different. With no words to their songs written down, I had to think of songs that I remembered from childhood (try to do that sometime), ones that the kids might know. After some negotiations, we settled on "Itsy Bitsy Spider," including hand gestures, and "Where Is Thumbkin?" which can also get quite boisterous. In a few minutes, these well-structured children, in their orderly, very tall power sitting positions, had been transformed into laughing little bodies, singing songs and rolling around on the floor. That might have been the day I fell in love with teaching.

Gina's Ride

During my years subbing, I spent a good deal of time at one of my small town's middle schools, where I became familiar and friendly with both the children and the staff. One of the duties included with subbing at that school was departure supervision, standing out in front of the school and watching the students as they walked home or were picked up, ensuring as best we could that they got home safely. One bright sunny day, a young vice principal named Arthur was already in position when I arrived.

Between him and me, our favorite topic of discussion was cars. Though it was all in good fun, what we particularly enjoyed doing was one-upping each other. I'm sure he knew I had just bought a brand-new Datsun, and when I came out to my position, he asked me, "So, Mr. Murphy, which ride is yours?"

I looked out over the parking lot and proudly answered, "Mine's the dark brown Datsun 200SX with the tinted windows. Which one is yours?"

He covered his eyes to shade them from the sun, pointed, and replied, "Mine's the blue Mazda with the spoiler."

As Arthur and I were bantering back and forth, a young girl named Gina walked up and, looking up to us, quietly waited to be included in our discussion. Smiling down at her, Arthur asked her, "So what's your ride these days, Gina?"

Without pausing, Gina pointed out across the parking lot to the bus loading zone and replied, "Mine's the yellow one with the black stripe and a chauffeur."

As my substituting career went on, I compiled a list of teachers who had enough control of their class to make subbing for them a really nice experience, and that is not always the case. Some teachers have no control of their classes whatsoever, and subbing for them can be a nightmare (a lesson well learned, more on classroom management and discipline later).

Fortunately, or unfortunately for me, the call I got and the eventual job I was offered was at the high school level, not elementary or middle school. However, I brought my lessons learned with me.

CHAPTER 5

Q: What Is It Like to Be a Student?

A: They are under everyone's control but their own.

OUR STUDENTS ARE OUR "kids," a beautiful compilation of our civilization, our ambitions, and our concerns bundled up and crammed into the unnatural worlds of both school and adolescence. It's a hard time for them, at least they think so, and anyone in education who does not truly empathize with and love these young people should consider a change in career, maybe become a plumber.

That said, students and their families are directly affected by their social and economic circumstances, and when students come to school, they leave a home environment where they are learning how to navigate these dynamics and finding out for themselves which actions will likely get them what they want or need. They watch their parents and others at home and learn in no uncertain terms what their family and community values and what it expects from them. Children inherently want to please those they like and those they know like them. Students bring this habit or talent for adapting with them into the classroom. Some of these children are the first generation of their family to be born in America. Some came from overseas or somewhere else. These first or second-generation American students may be even more embarrassed by their parents' social ignorance and lack of "hipness" than native-born teenagers are. And if they are used to getting away with challenging or disrespecting their authority figures at home, or making a cute or pouty face, or creating a scene in an attempt to get what they want, teachers will see this in the classroom. If it works for them in their real lives, children will fully expect it to work with their teachers. The veteran observer will see in a very few days exactly which faces or expressions work most consistently for the children at home. Then whatever face is used, if it is not directly useful to your lesson plan, point it out when they make it. Have the student make the face again so everyone in the room can see it and also see that if they make their own most useful face, they can expect that you will point theirs out to everyone as well. In short, if they are using a tool that has always worked for them and if you call them out on it and turn it around on them, they and every other child in the room will learn that that ploy to control their environment doesn't work with you.

However, students can just as likely be emotionally fragile souls. If things are going rough for them in their home life or socially at school, a critical word from a teacher, especially one they like, can set their emotions crashing or spinning out of control. So just be careful.

Students today are in a situation where they think they have very little control of their lives in any way. Besides their fully defined roles at home, the counselors and the school's graduation requirements control what classes they take and when they take them. And if they ask to change that schedule after they receive it, they are refused. (We have 2,400 students, and we cannot change all their schedules.)

In the classroom, the teacher creates the atmosphere and tells the students where to sit, what assignments are to be done, and when the assignments are due, not to mention that students are constantly being judged or "evaluated" on everything they do. And we have all seen the movies and have experienced our own examples of how cruel or confusing the social whirl of school can be. In short, they are not really sure just what they should be doing, and everything they do is controlled and/or criticized by themselves or by someone else. If you can remember how emotional or frustrating it felt to be a student, then that is a good place for a career as a teacher or administrator to begin.

In my student days, I was never the kid who sat in the front and had my hand up to answer questions. Many teachers were that kid. I would always opt for the seat in the back and ask the question that would get the teacher off the subject—what I now call a bomb thrower—ready for the thrill of blowing up the teacher's planned activity for that day. It was a fun game then, and now it makes me laugh when I see one of my kids sitting in the back, trying desperately to come up with just the right question that is close enough to the topic at hand to avoid being recognized as an obvious troublemaker; yet it's also a question that creates a rabbit hole for the teacher/ me to follow Alice into. Knowing firsthand what they're doing is helpful in avoiding the problem. You have a lot of material to cover and never enough time, so when this possible distraction happens, you must immediately call the bomb thrower on what they are doing. "Thank you, Mr. Jones. But if you will stay with the rest of us, we can all finish and cover the material we need to." It's fun for them if the student instigator can pull something over on the authority figure and get away with it. I have to admit, though, that every once in a while, a student bomb thrower will sit at the back of my classroom and ask just the right off subject question that beckons me down the rabbit hole; sometimes I choose to go there with them. Sure, it may not be strictly on the agenda, but maybe it's something close enough that others in the room would get something from the trip. It might be fun. And sometimes, the questioning is done cleverly enough to gain my respect as one former practitioner to the younger generation. "Well played." Sometimes you just have to lighten up.

A personal win.

Marcus Has His Moment

Marcus looked like a young Ozzy Osbourne—long dark hair parted down the middle of his scalp and hanging to his shoulders. And for the past two grading periods that year, beyond attending because the school and the police get involved if he doesn't, Marcus had shown no interest in doing schoolwork or in getting involved with the class. He was a clever and intelligent young man, and I liked him, but our agendas were not the same. Then I made a diverse project list of twentieth-century icons from around the world for my students to write a report on and to present to the class. The list included Pete Seeger and the Beatles from music, Ronald Reagan and Richard Nixon from politics, along with international leaders such as Hitler, Michael Gorbachev, Margaret Thatcher, and others. The students were assigned to pick one, write a five-page paper, and present their project to the class.

Marcus asked to add a name to the list, The Rolling Stones. Surprised he was thinking of doing anything, I quickly agreed. Three weeks later, when it was time to present, Marcus volunteered to present first. He started out playing "Sympathy for the Devil" on his iPod and then proceeded to describe the rise and development of the group from their early days through the drug busts and the death of Brian, through the music on successive albums, to his experience with his mother at a recent local concert by the Stones. As he spoke, his eyes, voice, and mannerisms showed excitement and enthusiasm. It turns out Marcus was also a musician, and he expressed his love for music and his personal knowledge of the history of the group, scoring the maximum on my presentation rubric. For that moment, Marcus had engaged, and a teacher's day was made.

Six years later, Marcus came to visit. Now he wears glasses and a beard that makes him look very much like Johnny Depp, or more precisely, Captain Jack Sparrow. He works, but making music is still the center of his life as he and his friends play guitar, make recordings, and try to break into that world. In short, he seems really happy.

Love for our kids is why teachers become teachers, and the highlight of our careers is seeing our kids succeed and be happy adults. However, it seems that every year, it gets harder to remember why we chose this life. Year after year, talented people examine their options and leave the profession. Eventually, the schools will be seen to be both unproductive and too expensive. If we continue to create a world where teachers, who are trying desperately to help create the productive and mentally creative citizens of tomorrow, are disrespected and fought with at every step, we will lose them—, at first, the teachers and then the schools themselves. We need to reverse this trend; however, society will decide.

CHAPTER 6

Q: Teaching—What Am I Stepping Into?

A: You are going to where you are desperately needed.

THE SCHOOL ENVIRONMENT—TEACHERS WITH their bachelor's or master's degree and the years of graduate school required to get a credential are among the most highly educated people in America, if not the world. And instead of using that education to sit in a cubicle and crunch numbers for some corporate report, their education and talents will be used to help young people envision and then achieve their dreams. It's thrilling. Being a teacher is an honor and a responsibility. However, it's not easy, and these bright young teachers are not here by chance. They have worked hard and have earned the right to walk on campus, and we need them. We need Superman, Batman, Wonder Woman, and all the others. In short, we need the superheroes these young people were trained to be.

And there are rewards. One day, years from now, hopefully, a young person like Marcus will walk back into your classroom and tell you that when they were in school, you showed them a kindness, taught them something, or that your very presence and attitude toward life made a life-changing difference to them. That's a feeling you will not get in corporate America, so have some fun. Yes, you're about to find out that being a teacher is the greatest job a person could ever have, but it's not all polished apples and teacher appreciation days.

To begin with, schools today are enclaves of defiant optimism, struggling to maintain and promote a wholesome, peaceful world. And it is a struggle. The world outside is getting harder to deal with every day. The scenario we face in school is very much like the ecological situation where an established productive fish population becomes prey for another invasive fish species who then replaces them, absorbs available resources, but does not contribute back to society. At first, the harmful element constitutes only a small fragment of the population, and no one really cares. We even find them charming in their differewnce. Eventually, when the invaders displace the traditional population and people dependent on the waterway and those original fish species realize that something is horribly wrong, they hopefully begin taking steps to fix the problem.

That's the point we are at today. In schools, we have a dwindling percentage of the traditional "good kid" population, most of whom come to us from parents who have established at home that they support the schools and that they have expectations that their children will not only avoid being a distraction in their classrooms but also thrive and benefit from their school experience. I call these traditional children the "beloved of God." Their names are Alejandra, Mark, Carlos, Maria, Nancy, MoNiq, D'Andra, Tuyen, Tram, Barbara, Thomas, and thousands of others. These children come to school, get there on time, and learn because that is not only what their parents expect but also what they expect of themselves. However, this traditional world environment can exist only as long as the majority of students come from homes where parents see school and what their kids are learning there as having value and where the parents enforce a code of compliance on their children because it is important to the children, to the family, and to their future.

Undoubtedly, today the American culture is getting rougher; the invasive elements are arriving in our classrooms in larger numbers every year. Make no mistake— American culture is undergoing a process of change, leaving even the best schools in a pinch between traditional structures and the demands of a new society. And why is that? For some families, even for the middle class living in America today, it can be very difficult for people to keep up with the increasing costs and other pressures of surviving, let alone raising a family, and a growing number of parents often working two or more jobs to live up to their responsibilities but without the technological training required for today's better paying jobs find their personal lives so challenging that they give up and surrender to the children themselves the very demanding duty of parenting. It's not a scientifically based study, but I asked my students, "How many of you know someone who works two or more jobs just to get by?" Nearly half of the kids present raised their hands. These people are trying to do what is best for their children, trying to be the parents their children need, but it can become an overwhelming task. And some parents simply don't spend time looking for more problems to be solved from an institution like school that they think should safely take care of their children for a time and hopefully send them home with fewer problems than they had before.

Because there's a law saying that children must be in school, these struggling parents force their kids to go. But the children know what is going on. They can come to believe that their getting to school every day is only important because their parents will face problems with law enforcement if they do not attend. But they also know that there is nothing in the law that says they have to buckle under and learn anything. Instead of joining a voluntary process that we belonged to in days past, these children feel that they are being forced to enter a repressive system that demands of them their time but whose family and social group don't believe provides them with enough in return. That new viewpoint changes the school environment from one of children actively learning in their own self-interest to one of "Okay, I'm forced to be here. I'm here, so entertain me." Predictably, these children with minimal home expectations are less likely to perform or behave as required in their classrooms, especially if the teacher dares to raise the bar of expectations.

And the progress reports sent home by the school

as a means of updating the parents and, in some cases, asking for their help are seen by the parents as yet another unappreciated message that just adds pressure and expectations to their lives. Sometimes this notification or the child's concern for his parents' negative reaction to it will cause notable positive reactions. Usually, it doesn't. In fact, what happens all too often is that the child, having gotten home earlier than their parents, intercepts the progress report that was mailed home, and the parents, who are not looking for new problems in their lives to handle, do not follow up and ask where the reports are, let alone call the school and find out the bad news. In recent years, with the availability of such Internet programs as "Schoolloop" and other 24/7 updates to all the child's grades, it's only a matter of a few button clicks for parents to keep up with their children's success or lack of success in school and to do it online. But the parent still has to be motivated to take those steps and then handle the problem with the child. They have to be willing to add new concerns to their already hectic lives. Increasing numbers of individual parents just don't do it.

These parents ask their child, "How's school going?"

And they accept the answer "Okay."

Or if they ask if the child has done their homework,

they let it drop when the child looks up from their texting and responds, "I didn't have any."

As for what parents, to people outside the system and society in general want from the schools, it's simple: they themselves don't want to take on increasing individual burdens concerning the morality or expectations of their children themselves. They want the schools to take responsibility for that. They pay their tax money and literally want the schools to prepare their children to join society as good people and to also be able to make a living by contributing something to that society. However, the schools don't see these goals as their primary functions. The schools see their responsibility limited to the academic subjects included in a liberal arts education that finds its fulfillment in literacy, mathematics, science, and a dash of critical thinking. The teachers say, "I wish the parents would get a clue as to what their child is doing and fix it before they bring their problems to school. All the while, parents point to the schools as failing their kids. Put bluntly, the schools and the parents point to each other, both unhappy with the performance of the other; the child plays both sides against each other for their own immediate reasons, and many children drop through the cracks.

To continue the fish in the stream analogy, the environment of any school directly reflects not only the combined experience of the children but also the surrounding neighborhoods. If the students in our classes have learned to read and write and have gained a sense of personal discipline, that can make our job far easier. If, on the other hand, the children have been "socially promoted" through the system or have recently migrated here and come to our classrooms without the basic skills of reading and writing in English (and people outside education would be surprised how many students, even students who were born in the United States, come to school in just that condition) or if the immediate area around the school is a deteriorating section of the inner city or is gang-or crack house-infested or if their parents are chronically unemployed or underemployed and there are no social structures available to help them, those issues and worse will seep into our environment. The pollution of the outside world will pollute our streams. Children do not learn when they are afraid or hungry, and can we expect them to put the necessary effort into learning when their neighborhood and the lives of their parents and relatives tell them every day that no matter how much they learn in school, they will never have a chance? Last year, when he was in eleventh grade, one of my favorite kids in the world, a Hispanic student, told me very proudly that though he was down some units toward graduation from when he messed up as a freshman and sophomore, he had been planning his future with his counselor and that if he didn't fail any more classes, he was going to graduate from high school after all, which was a big deal because "nobody in my whole family has ever graduated. I'll be the first."

As it is today, the invasive population, which can only be called a roughening of our culture, is growing quickly. Like so much in our society, what we hold most dear, or not, can best be illustrated in terms of money. When state budgets get cut, schools, being among the largest expenses at the state level, can be an early target for quick cutting. However, once the economy has rebounded, these cuts can take time to be reallocated. According to the Center on Budget Policy and Priorities (May 2014 by Michael Leachman and Chris Mai) on our history of lingering educational budget cuts:

> The reduced levels (in state budgets for education in 2014) reflect not only the lingering effects of the 2007-2009 recession

but also continued austerity in many states; indeed, despite some improvements in overall state revenues, schools in around a third of states are entering the new school year with less state funding than they had last year.

It's completely counterintuitive, but even though most people agree that education is the key to a better tomorrow for all of us, education is simply not our top national priority. I am a lifelong Conservative Republican, and to me, that means that national defense should be the first and most important responsibility of government. But enough is enough, and then we become irresponsibly wasteful. The American taxpayers spent 18 percent of the federal budget on Defense in 2015, a total of $610 billion according to the Stockholm International Peace Research Institute. Before questioning if that number to protect our country is high enough, understand that in 2015 we outspent the next seven countries combined in defense spending, and five of those seven are our longtime allies. (According to the SIP National Priorities Project, the amount spent was actually $598 billion or roughly 54 percent of federal discretionary spending.) Granted, the next two largest spending countries, Russia and China, are threats, but if we merely *matched their combined* expenditure for weaponry, we could save $300 billion a year, every year. We could cut taxes for the working poor and give parents more money to survive on. Or we could spend that $300 billion per year on day care for working moms or for advanced training centers for dads or moms or anyone else whose skills do not fill the needs of an increasing technical economy, making it easier for parents to devote more time to raising their children, the leaders of tomorrow. On the other hand, we could spend some of that money to reinstate programs in school like the arts, music, or for vocational programs that teach working skills that actually help students prepare to be adults and to make the time spent in school rewarding. To paraphrase a well-known bumper sticker of the late '60s, "What if the schools got all the money they needed to prepare our children for the future and the military had to have bake sales?" Though steps were taken to help him personally and academically, my student continued coming to school but stopped putting in the effort. This year he came by to tell me he had failed some classes and that he would not be graduating with his class. Sadly, for his family, the cycle continues.

Our national priorities can be frustrating, but standing

up for and working hard for these children can also be what motivates us. Most teachers want to be saviors, the ones who reach down into the mire and confusion of society and gently help lift the children to a safer, better future. It's in our DNA. It's who we are. But we practice our trade in a world where the surrounding communities' attitude about the value of the education we provide is dwindling, as is their respect for authority, specifically for teachers. Gone are the days when a child would hear a question, raise their hand, wait to be acknowledged, and then stand and answer.

Socioeconomically, my school is majority Hispanic and Asian, with a household income spread reaching from country club to rough East side neighborhood. Approximately 35 to 45 percent of our kids are on the assisted or free lunch programs. We have gangs, but the efforts of the administration and the local city police departments have generally kept representation and problems away from our classrooms. In general, we don't have the horrific problems other schools have, such as guns on campus and angry students attacking or threatening their teachers. These things happen, but they don't happen everywhere.

CHAPTER 7

Q: Who Are These Children and How
Did They Get That Way?

A: These children are the disrespectful,
entitled, and disconnected people we
have trained them to be.

WHO THESE CHILDREN ARE is simple—
they are our children, and like us, they are the
product of the generations who came before them. In
our classrooms, they can appear to be disconnected,
expectant, disrespectful, and entitled people who want
only to be entertained. But nature didn't produce them
that way; we did. The story of today's students begins in
the late 1930s and early 1940s, long before they were born,

when Franklin Roosevelt maneuvered the United States into World War II. Between 1941 and 1945, trained by our armed forces and chomping at the bit to kill Nazis and Japs, roughly fifteen million men of reproductive age departed for the European or Pacific theaters of war, leaving another fifteen million fertile young women alone and frustrated. When the men returned home after years of experiencing the killing and bloodshed of war, they created what has become known as the baby boom, my people. But the nuclear firestorms over Hiroshima and Nagasaki that ended their conflict were only firecrackers compared to the social and political explosion that shook the 1960s and which has shaped the decades and generations since.

According to researcher and writer Tim Madigan in his work on the psychic suffering of WWII vets (*The Week*):

> More than 1 million Americans who fought in that conflict were discharged for psychoneurotic disorders. By 1947, nearly half of the beds in Veterans Administration hospitals were filled with men with Post-Traumatic Stress Disorder. A suppressed

1946 documentary by director John Houston reported that 20 percent of US casualties suffered primarily psychic, not physical wounds that left them with night terrors, survivor's guilt, depression and alcoholism. The brutal reality of what that war did to veteran's psyche have been lost amid the mythology of the Greatest Generation.

When US Air Force Second Lieutenant Joseph Murphy returned from the war, he married June Johnson, and they made their seven contributions to the baby boom. However, the world travel that had come with the world war and the ensuing killing that their generation, the Greatest Generation, committed and witnessed in the conflict in addition to the separation from what they knew had changed them. How could it not? According to the National WWII Museum, 418,500 Americans, 418,700 British, 3.1 million Japanese, 24 million Soviets, and hundreds of thousands of others from other countries died in that war.

In the version of normal that the Greatest Generation inherited from their parents, the children of the Great Depression, and the normal that the returning warriors expected to continue, grown- up people got married and had children (strictly in that order). White-collar working men were expected to dress in gray suits and white shirts with thin black ties, carry briefcases, and go off to work, hopefully in some large corporation like GM, Ford, or in the Aerospace industry where they could work their way up the corporate ladder, make enough to raise a family, and retire in modest comfort on a combination of a pension and the newly created Social Security system. Blue-collar workers had factories to go to where they, too, could work their whole adult life and get "at least as far as their old man got" (Billy Joel, "Allentown"). Then they, too, would spend their later years in comfort and security. Women were expected to follow the same path that women had always followed: reach puberty and get married, stay home and have babies, and follow the lead of June Cleaver and Donna Reed (a string of pearls, a dress, and heels while vacuuming). Sex was not for pleasure but was a woman's obligation to create new life. Divorce was a mortal sin, and abortions were illegal, too often done in dark alleys and could be deadly. But our parents not only defeated both the Nazis and the Imperial Japanese Army but also came home and planted the seed of discontent with that norm within their children, who went on to wreak havoc on history.

We, the baby boomers, were the first to live under the cloud of the atomic bomb. We grew up knowing that all it would take was for some fool, in either Washington DC or Moscow, to push a button, and we could all die. We knew it and feared it all our lives, and in the Cuban Missile Crisis in 1962, the leaders of the world went eyeball to eyeball and nearly did get us all killed. Over and over, President Kennedy came onto our television sets to update us as we came closer and closer to nuclear war.

In addition to our newly formed generational understanding that mankind now had the technical means to kill everyone on the planet, we also had the overriding experience that people in authority, if it was in their self-interest to keep us occupied and calm, would lie to us or withhold information. Hiding under a school desk would keep us occupied during mandatory atomic bomb drills at school. It would frighten us into obedience, but doing as we were told would not keep us safe from a nuclear blast. We were not stupid, and we figured out that the action was futile and that they were lying. We also came to understand that there was something else wrong in the larger society, something that parents in that era did not tell their children about. For our parents, the children of the Great Depression, and the warriors of WWII, it was neither manly nor acceptable for men to complain about their duties and responsibilities nor to express the internal pressures they were feeling. They were expected to maintain "a stiff upper lip." We did, however, watch our fathers drink bottle after bottle of Mylanta for the peptic ulcers caused by the pressures they were under. Both men and women were placed in an impossible situation. For them, there was no standing up to what was grinding them down. "Taking it like a man" was simply a part of what their society expected of them. "Taking your lumps" was what both men and women were expected to do. Quoting the Madigan article again about the returning warriors:

> The deepest wound was right here, one veteran, Earl Crumby told me, as he pointed to his head. Another veteran, Otis Mackey, said "When we got out, you couldn't talk about things like that. Instead, he and others suffered in silence, convinced they were alone. But even the 'good war' did terrible things to those who fought it."

In time, it became clear to the boomer generation that living the life imposed on them by society created more stress than was healthy for our parents to carry. In retrospect, we did not really understand what our parents were going through, but as their marriages began to dissolve and their health deteriorated (Joe and June divorced after twenty three years together, and both died too young), the clear message that remained was that they were not happy. And as a result, it made us think that there must be a better way to live our lives. And to our credit, the baby boomers did take responsibility for the choices available to them. They encountered resistance from the reigning power structure, yet they chose to change the world around them.

During the 1960s, when I was between eight and eighteen years old, we were lied to again about what would become the largest cause of civil unrest in our generation, the war in Vietnam, which, contrary to all official reports at the time, we were not winning. Lies by the President, the generals, and other government officials added to a deepening distrust of authority and of society that the radicalized children of the 1950s were already feeling. Our parents generally supported the government and its version of the truth, as they always had. We came to question everything.

The baby boomers, coming of age, rejected our fathers'

shirts and ties and then let go of our parents and their society's sense of materialism, "keeping up with the Joneses," and "climbing the corporate ladder" in favor of "free love," drugs, spiritualism, and "living in the moment." We are called the baby boom because, during those formative years, there were more of us than any other generation. And because the United States was the unchallenged economic power in the world after the war, we as a generation had access to money—lots of money. We screamed our welcome to the British invasion led by the Beatles and bought millions of dollars' worth of records. We developed a culture of our own based on that wealth and the accompanying sense of independence. The capital of the new society was the Haight-Ashbury district of San Francisco. We grew our hair long, experimented with drugs, moved to rock music, and hoped to "die before I get old" (the Who. My Generation). Our philosopher kings were Bob Dylan and John Lennon. Woodstock, where thousands of young people came together and cared for each other in the spirit of love for three days without authority figures or adult supervision, became the days that showed our generation what might be possible. Essentially, we rejected everything our parents built their lives on—responsibility, the need for competition, and the whole "corporate thing"— opting instead for a generational mix of "All You Need Is Love," "The Times They Area Changin'," and a heavy dose of "You Are Not the Boss of Me." And because there were more of us than any other generation till that time, our voices would become *the* voice in both economics and politics. We were determined that our version of the possible, our rebellion against authority, would become reality.

However, during the 1960s, our possibly utopian ideals came up against a series of thunderous responses from what we would call "the real world." In 1963, John Kennedy, the youngest American President ever to serve and who, with his young wife and family, had come to personify for us the new generation of America, was assassinated. Then his assassin, Lee Harvey Oswald, was shot— actually murdered—while in police custody in Dallas, and he was murdered in front of all of us on national television. The man who killed the assassin, Jack Ruby, too conveniently died in jail of cancer before people were satisfied that the complete truth behind the assassination had become known. We wanted to know the truth. Who had really killed the President? There were facts, interpretations of apparent facts, and hundreds of questions and conspiracy theories. Had it been the Cubans with the help of their Russian masters who killed him, seeking revenge for the Bay of Pigs Invasion? Oswald had been known to frequent the Cuban embassy in Mexico, had travelled to Moscow, and had married a Russian wife. Had it been the mob who killed him because President Kennedy had been known to be having a relationship with the girlfriend of a mob boss? Or maybe the FBI was involved because J. Edgar Hoover reportedly hated the rich-kid Kennedys. Even the new President, Lyndon Johnson, who lived in Texas and who had fought John Kennedy for the Democratic nomination in 1960 and as a result of the assassination had actually reached his long-time goal of becoming president, was suspected. Perhaps Johnson, his Vice President, had played Brutus to Kennedy's Caesar? And who was the unknown figure on the grassy knoll?

Eventually, we were told by a Blue Ribbon group of trusted statesmen, the Warren Commission led by the Chief Justice of the United States, that no matter how many people questioned the version they settled on as the truth, the assassin Oswald was the killer, he had worked alone, and there was no more to it. Many of us thought that made no sense, and we wondered if our leaders were lying to us again. What truth was so heinous that they had to cover it up? In the following decades, whatever was covered up in the 1960s concerning the assassination has remained covered, and have died, the rest of us have had to resign ourselves to the fact that the truth might never surface.

In the spring of 1968, after the Civil Rights Act of 1964 and the Voting Rights Act of 1965 were signed into law, there was some glimmer of hope that the racial divide within America could be getting smaller and that maybe the nation might be healing after a hundred years of racial conflict. Dr. Martin Luther King Jr., then the world's most prominent Apostle of nonviolent protest, went to Memphis, Tennessee, to support garbage workers who were striking for respect as men and for a livable wage. On April 4, 1968, he was assassinated. Gone was the dreamer, and cities around America went up in flames, spawning rioting that was only put down by the National Guard and elements of the US Army using tear gas and bayonets.

In the 1960s, all of this was going on against the backdrop of a still expanding war in Vietnam, which had begun as a semi-popular war for democracy and against the evil of Communism. It was a surrogate war—pitting the communist-backed North Vietnamese against the

Western/Americanbacked South Vietnamese. Ascribing to the domino theory that if Vietnam were to fall to the Communists, the rest of Asia would fall as well, Kennedy had sent advisers and trainers into the fight. After the assassination, Johnson had escalated our involvement in the war to over five hundred thousand fighting troops. However, after years of raised and dashed hopes of victory against a collage of less virtuous and poorly armed Communist malefactors and with the coverage of the war in our homes on national television, America's ability to stomach the carnage waned. Young people, the ones who were scheduled to do the fighting overseas, began the rude work of questioning their elders and those in authority. "Hell no, we won't go." It was then that the political power of the generation raised its head. Even though the 26th Amendment to the Constitution, changing the voting age to eighteen, would not pass until 1971, many of the boomers were old enough to vote, and millions of others were willing to become politically active, especially challenging authority. The boomers would rally for peace and have walkouts and demonstrations on campuses all over the country, but would anyone with a chance to hold real world political power take up the cause and walk with them? The answer for a while seemed to be Bobby

Kennedy, the younger brother of the President, the former Attorney General, and Senator from New York. Senator Kennedy did pick up the peace mantle, became a viable candidate, and drove President Johnson from his bid for reelection. For us, things began to look possible. Perhaps the side of peace would prevail. Perhaps good would triumph over evil. Struggling within the political system after losing in the Oregon primary, Senator Kennedy won a crucial primary in California, garnering its huge delegate count, and looked forward to the Democratic Party National Convention in Chicago later that year.

The night of the primary, June 6, 1968, after having been named the victor, Bobby paused and thanked his followers and then walked through the kitchen of the Ambassador Hotel, where he had made his state headquarters. There, an assassin ended his life and the hope of young people across the country that peaceful change was possible. I was fifteen. Again we woke up in the morning, prepared to go to school, and got to watch Bobby's lifeless body in a pool of blood on the floor. Three men who had seemed to want to lead the new generation of Americans to a new frontier of peace and equality had died at the hand of assassins and were each buried while we watched on television.

But as it happens, we the hippies of the 1960s and those that wanted to be hippies eventually grew up, settled up in pairs, at least temporarily, and had our own children. That's when the lives of today's teachers were bound to be different. We, the boomers, wanting to avoid the stifling strict world of our parents, raised our children to be free with their feelings, expressive, verbal, and unafraid of failure or of anything else; we especially were not afraid of authority figures. We had money, so our children would want for nothing. We were, and still are, the generation who believes that it is not only healthy for society but also necessary for our freedom to challenge authority. Why would the schools expect the children and grandchildren we raised to blindly follow directions, raise their hands before speaking, or do something as miserably conventional as homework? Today, in our classrooms and at home, when confronted by authority, our children simply click off, mentally and emotionally disconnect, like they do when something that they don't like appears on their ever-present electronics. These children, our children and grandchildren, have become the nonproductive, self-centered, and entitled student body of today. And that is precisely who they are: self-centered and entitled. That is why the new teacher of today has to be above the past, a trailblazer motivated to reach them. It is why we cannot continue with the school structure that provided what was needed in past decades. Our children and their educational needs are different, and the schools they are trained in must also change dramatically.

CHAPTER 8

Q: So How Can the Schools and Teachers
        Deal with This?

A: Look at the basics.

FOR "HOW TO" ANSWERS, I go back to lessons I learned on my first days as a substitute. A child's feeling of personal security and a schedule that lets them know what will happen next are vital. The first step in educating children is to immediately establish a safe, appreciative, and empowering structure for each child yet with an expected school-wide norm that disturbing the class and denying other students the same opportunity to learn is rude, disrespectful to others, and will not be tolerated. The next principle our schools need to establish is a solid link between accomplishment and reward as compared to the lack of accomplishment and lack of reward. And like discipline, reward must also be both immediate and sure. Today's students need an immediate incentive to perform, one that has meaning to them. Children who do well on tests should be publicly recognized, their names announced and cheered. At the end of each grading period, those with A's and B's, the students who have done the work and have learned the material, should receive public acclaim for what they have achieved. This could be as simple as a T-shirt or a button proclaiming, "I'm a winner at XYZ School." Some schools now use bumper stickers to let parents show how proud they are of their children, but the reward should be something that the child who has accomplished the goal can wear with pride. This kind of reinforcement, if the students have truly earned it, can motivate and encourage them to future success, and future success is the name of the game. This certainly does *not* mean directly shaming those students who do not succeed. However, rewarding and encouraging students for success directly reflects what they will find when they graduate. We need these kids to be prepared to run the country they will inherit from us.

At the same time, there must be predictable and sure consequences for disrupters. They cannot be allowed to become "cool." As a school, we must establish a kind of normal that includes mutual respect and a chance for every child to learn. However, for some children, the idea of a controlled environment where they are not the focus of attention is not only foreign to them but also unacceptable. On individual occasions, disruptive behaviors can be addressed with a blend of certain rebuke of the disruption, respect for all (including the offender), and some humor. However, like the proverbial rotten apple, one disrupter allowed and unaddressed can become many. The invasive species will multiply and overtake the classroom and, if left to run its course, the school. Make no mistake, as our society becomes more progressive, more understanding of bad behavior, and less rigidly institutional, the disrupters' invasion of schools will continue. For example: within an hour's drive from my school, there are schools and whole school districts where the disrupters prevail, and the beloved of God have been driven out or silenced. It's just that simple. In those schools and school districts, disruption has become the norm. When that happens, productive students will flee.

With voucher systems being established in some states

and charter schools opening, successful students and their parents will make decisions about their futures. Successful students will leave for better academic environments and opportunities, high schools with reputations of excellence that will help get them accepted into high-ranking colleges. The existing administrators of the failing schools will come under increased pressure to raise performance scores, but without the cream-of-the-crop students, that becomes a more difficult thing for them to do. In addition, when turmoil descends on a school and when disrupters overpower the classrooms, what teachers are going to take a job working there? There's not enough money in the world. The most highly qualified and gifted teachers will not risk their safety nor put up with the other dangers and frustrations inherent in working in those schools. *And no, they do not have to.* An even worse result happens when the disrupters are empowered. They actually become "cool," soaking up available class time at the expense of the other students who do not get a fair chance to learn. Finally, the total environment of the school continues to deteriorate. Predictably, if no teachers or administrators want to work under those conditions, they will demand more money to do so, but school budgets are limited, and in time these schools cannot pay enough to adequately staff their classrooms.

Furthermore, when failure brings predictions of future failure, which then come true, the students, administrations, and surrounding community can lose what little respect they have left for the teachers and staff who remain, as the parents and children at those low-performing schools come to the logical conclusion that their children's school conditions are declining because the teachers who do agree to work in their schools, those who are not talented enough to get a job at a "good" school, are to blame, and the spiral down continues.

Already disadvantaged, the teachers these schools need most, the really good ones, will be the first ones drawn away to other districts or out of education completely. Highly educated people have choices. And again, over the years, the problems in these schools go from bad to worse.

The scary truth is that to some extent, this same scenario, where social problems, especially disrespect for teachers and the value of what the education system offers them and a disconnect between reward and sure discipline, is taking root and growing, making teaching more and more difficult on its way to impossible almost everywhere. On their way to quitting the profession after twenty or more years, two highly respected teachers summed it up this way: first, "I became a teacher because I wanted to lead my students up the hill, and I have always loved that. Now I'm expected to push them up the hill dragging and screaming, and I didn't sign up for that." Second, "Simply, I'm leaving teaching because I don't want to be frustrated and angry all the time." This hopefully sobering truth is a large part of why, even after all the years of work they put in to become a teacher, almost half of all teachers quit teaching during their first five years. It's a lot to put up with, and it's getting worse. Why should educated and talented people stay? Why should they put up with it?

However, it's not only poor or disadvantaged schools that have problems. On the other end of the financial spectrum, rich schools in wealthy neighborhoods have issues with their community as well. Far from the lack of achievement experienced in some schools, these parents have a history of succeeding at almost everything and of getting exactly what they want. These parents can also get so involved in surviving their own lives that child-centered parental guidance of their children becomes secondary. At a school just north of my workplace, there have been six student suicides in the last few years, generally blamed on pressures students feel to achieve in high school. These parents have raised the expectation bar very much higher than their children's own aspirations. Though there are few obviously dilapidated crack houses in these neighborhoods, other social problems exist. And often, the problem of lack of respect for authority is compounded by a matter of high expectations. For instance, some parents have set the expectation bar so high for their children, not just getting into college but more so getting into Stanford or Harvard that they and their children will forget or toss out all the other social values, like telling the truth, scholastic integrity, and respect for themselves and for people around them. They and, thus, their children will lie, cheat, and badger the teacher into allowing misbehavior and into changing grades from what the child's work earns to what they need to keep their GPA stellar. Even in one of my favorite movies, *The Blind Side,* with Sandra Bullock, we see Mama (Bullock), a very rich Southern woman, asking her son's English teacher, "All his other teachers are on board. I don't know what *your problem* is... Michael needs a B, what does he have to do to deserve that?" when Michael needs a higher grade to graduate from high school and then to get him into an NCAA college to play football. After being badgered by the rich parent and star of the movie, the English teacher sets a limited yet achievable goal for Michael; and with considerable work from others on his behalf, including a personal live-in tutor, the paper gets written and the grade achieved. The audience applauds Mama's perseverance and accomplishment in getting her son the grade he needs, but did Michael ever learn to think logically, or was he even the one who wrote the paper? In the movie, Michael is heard reading the finished paper, but did he write the paper himself? Just after Michael gets credit for the paper and qualifies to graduate with the necessary grade, Bullock is again applauded for breaking into the school's computer and then deceiving the school staff by entering a baby picture of Michael for his graduation ceremony that was not even him. In fact, the only writing that we know Michael actually did himself was to put his signature on a contract with the NFL's Ravens. So good job, Mom, and we hope Michael is still okay. (But is that what we want for Michael and our other kids?) As an update, Michael Oher went on to play for the Tennessee Titans and then to the Carolina Panthers. In October of 2016, he was benched according to NFL concussion protocols, and in August of 2017, he was cut from the Panthers, having failed his physical.

Parents and the outside community can lose sight of the fact that the benefit students are meant to gain from the experience of either public or private education is not only in recalling bits of data. Their electronics can do that. Nor is it only about getting grades in order to be judged worthy at some higher level. There are important acquired skills in being able to understand an assignment, to then get mentally organized, and in getting the product done. There's an additional value to students in learning to get somewhere on time, having their work done on time, and writing like an educated person. If our kids don't acquire the skills needed to do the things they are asked to do in high school, they are not likely to be prepared to compete if or when they get to their destination school, let alone a work environment.

With some of my teacher-friends who work in upscale schools, especially in private church-affiliated schools, stories like this are all too common. Edward and his class are given a project to do and directions as to how to do it. When he turns it in, Edward's project shows a complete lack of effort and a disregard for the instructions given. In short, it's a mess and deserves a failing grade, which is what the teacher gives it. The next day, the teacher is called to the principal's office to meet with Edward's mother, where she (the teacher) must defend herself and justify why the grade was so low. Even after the project and the directions are reviewed and the quality of the work is shown to be wanting, the mother insists the grade be changed because it drops the child's grade point average for college. The principal's initial stance is to remain neutral, partly in support of the teacher and the school's academic standing and perhaps partly in deference to the large amount of money the parent pays to have Edward come to that school. Since most private schools do not have strong unions to protect the people working there, this teacher knows that her continued employment is determined by the future good will of the principal, who at that moment would rather not have to deal with a situation that was apparently caused by this teacher. Eventually, the parent persists, the principal defers, and the teacher is pressured to back away from her standards. The grade gets changed, reaffirming within hours what every other student and parent at that school knows. Grades can and will be changed if the parents go over the head of the teacher to the principal. And parents and students will do just that. After all, it's their school; they pay for it. The results are that the mother feels she succeeded in her mission; the grade is what she needs it to be. On the negative side, Edward gains no skills and has an unrealistic view of how the world works. (In the future, Mom will not be able to badger his boss to rehire him when Edward gets fired for being nonproductive, but Mom and Edward will wonder together why everyone is so mean to him.) As for the teacher, she is frustrated, feels cheapened, and mentally measures her distance to the exit door.

Like new teachers today, most people I know came to teaching out of true altruism. They came to education to help their students grow in their subject matter because they love it and to help develop our children into good people with a moral code and a sense of ethics. But when it's the parents who come to fight the teacher when the student performs poorly or to prevent any kind of deserved consequence from befalling their child should they be caught cheating or committing some other infraction, how can teachers cope with that? Over time, it is far easier for a teacher to just give in, decide not to risk their current and future income, and assign the student a grade the work does not deserve. It's against the teacher's morality and sense of right and wrong. It cheapens the whole school experience for both this child and all future children, but it's not their kid. Why should dedicated teachers lose sleep to do the right thing? Why should they have to fight? However, the parents who demand that their children be passed, even if their work does not earn them the right to do so, are the same parents who will damn the schools and the teachers if their child actually reaches Stanford or Harvard, or anyplace else for that matter, and is not prepared to succeed.

My own favorite story in this vein is the time I got summoned to the principal's conference room to talk to the parent of a child who had been in my class *the previous year*. I have approximately 165 kids every year, but I did remember the boy because no matter how I tried to get him to do anything that year, including one-on-one discussions and moving him to the front of the class in case it was a vision problem, still he had sat there and had done nothing for two semesters as a junior. Now he was a senior, and Mom was interested in him graduating. My class was US History and was required for graduation. In a conference room with her son, the principal, and myself, she asked, visibly angry, "How could you have given my son an F?" Fortunately, my school has a system called Schoolloop that records every grade a student earns for every assignment and makes that information available 24/7 online. In preparation for this meeting, I ran his grades to show his mother the long line of zeroes that added up to his F grade. Mom was unimpressed with the record. She insisted it was my fault that the boy failed because I had not personally called her to tell her that her son was not doing well. "That was your incompetence as a teacher," she said.

"Mrs. X, you were sent six report cards over that time and had Schoolloop available to you 24/7. If you had looked at any of them, you would have known. When do you think it becomes your responsibility to keep up on your son's grades?"

And then my favorite parental quote: "All his other teachers called me!" she shouted.

"Really, Mrs. X, you knew he was failing all of his classes, and you were waiting for a call from me before you did something about it?" I'm absolutely sure that these parents loved their kids, but if they prove their love by fighting other authority figures in their lives who are doing their best to help the kids develop into responsible human beings, what are the kids learning? And how is that preparing them for their future?

The difference between my case and that of my friends

at private schools is that I knew that the only person who could legally force me to change my grade, according to the California Education Code (the legal Bible in public schools in California), was the district superintendent, and that even if my principal wanted to threaten my job, my union would have supported me. In the end, the grade was not changed, and the mother left, threatening to go to the district. I don't know if she ever did.

It can help keep a teacher's head from exploding if they can remember this one thing: whatever the disrupters are doing, even if they are doing it in your classroom, it likely has very little to do with you personally. Though when you have worked on a lesson plan and these children are ruining it, it's difficult to remember that it is not something they are doing against you. Unfortunately, that does not make it any less frustrating.

Another thing to remember as the only authority figure in the classroom is that even with today's best students, when you catch them in the act or have indisputable evidence that they have done something wrong, like cheating, they will act surprised, deny it unless you have concrete proof, and even when you do have the proof, they will tearfully plead that it's their first time ever doing anything wrong and as such you should forgive them. A more likely truth is: nothing happened for the first time today.

The child you catch cheating today has very likely been doing it for years and has always gotten away with it. And they expect you to let them as well. Also, the way the child behaves in your class is exactly what they do in all their other classes. If they lie or cheat or if they sit and do nothing in your class today, this has likely been their pattern for years. Children, like most people, continue doing what has worked for them in the past.

Many, many students today have learned to play the "I'll exert only enough energy to not get into trouble with the teacher or my parents" game for their whole lives. At home, it's why it can take them hours or even days to clean up their rooms (until the parent or other authority figure at home presents them with a reward or a consequence). In the classroom, it often happens that though they appear to be doing something when you look at them, rarely does any work get turned in. For these students, it is a game. In their eyes, they have experienced the fun of gambling, and they have won. They have expended no energy, and they did not get into trouble.

When a teacher recognizes this and when addressing it with the child makes no difference, it's time to involve the parents. But a call home from a teacher will not likely fix the problem. The child knows their parents far better than their school does, and they know how their parents will react or if they will do anything besides looking exasperated and tired. And many parents are tired of the whole mess. Parents can get call after call like this from their child's teachers each grading period, and nothing they say or do seems to make any difference. To the teacher, it may be a new day, but for the parents, it is a continuing history of still another problem that they do not want to contend with. Consequently, when I call, the parents are often even more exasperated with the child than I am. And though the teacher has the child for an hour each school day, they have him or her 24/7 and have for years.

I sometimes hear a tired sadness in the parent's voice. "Okay, what have they done now?" Sometimes a call or message home will spur a big change, but usually not. But if we care about these kids, we cannot just make the call and let the subject drop. Statistics show that people who do not graduate from high school, even if at fourteen to eighteen they don't see the need and that they do, in fact, face a lifetime of unnecessary poverty and hardship. And we are not talking about students with identifiable handicaps. Those children usually work as hard as they can and want to learn. What bothers parents and teachers as well are the cases where the child can do the work but simply refuses to participate. "You are not the boss of me." (Sounds familiar?) But neither their parents nor their teachers want to give up on them. We continually struggle to find a way to connect with them. But it's not easy, neither is it always fun.

CHAPTER 9

Q: How Do You Keep Control with That Many Students?

A: By being clear and consistent.

IN THE CLASSROOM IS where we succeed or fail and the stakes are high. And though it does take a village to raise a child, it's the teacher who will be in the classroom every day and who will be held responsible for delivering the curriculum and evaluating the student's success. Every school day, there are over 165 students moving through my classroom and those of most other teachers, and if we are going to have the best chance for that many children to succeed, everyone must understand that the only adult in the room is the one in charge.

Students generally expect that to be the case, at least to the extent that parental authority is practiced at home. And there are ways to reinforce the *authority* message and to do so in a way that focuses everyone's attention on what needs to be accomplished and yet does not diminish the child's creativity.

Today's children are very good at picking up messages. But how do we help them understand that learning to deal with people with the authority to help them or hold them to performance standards is a fact of life (even when these people do not necessarily love them like their parents and friends do)? It is the way the world is. Students today need to understand (even come to value) that it's for their own good that their teachers hold them accountable for their performance. Beyond that, children need to learn that the ability to cope with and then the ability to do well in a demanding circumstance now and in their future (or not) will have serious benefits or consequences for them. In that regard, ground zero is the teacher, and in the classroom, the children have what may be their first opportunity to learn this most basic of lessons: there are and will be people in their lives whom they must respect, if only because these people have the authority (or ability) to help or hinder their progress and their future. Even if they don't think they are learning anything that is valuable enough to justify the hours of school they are required to attend, this lesson can be a beginning.

The appearance of authority in their school environment can begin with something as simple as the placement of desks in the classroom. It's not a coincidence that the teacher's desk is large and up at the focal point of the room and the student desks are much smaller. It's an unmistakable symbol of power. Who is in charge here? As to the placement of student desks in my room, I copied from one of my mentors, Mr. G, leaving a roughly two desk- wide walkway down the middle of the room and rows of three or four desks facing each other on each side. This way, the teacher is never more than four desks away from observing any student. The student will be given a growing amount of freedom as they earn it by achieving our goals, but the teacher is the responsible party, and the children will not be unobserved.

Two more tools can be used to demonstrate that the adult is in charge: first, on the very first day of class, I tell my incoming students that they can sit anywhere they choose, "but if you sit next to someone who will get you in trouble, I'll be moving you" (i.e., you will make choices in this class, but the room is still mine). Second, the standard of conduct must be established. Children want to know what is expected of them, and it adds to their feelings of security. The first day of class, the first time they meet the teacher, is the best day to establish those expectations. Just after I warmly greet them and welcome them, I hand out a written list titled "Class Rules" or "How We Are All Going to Get Along This Year," and we read it together. I first remind them that this class (in my case, US History, Economics, or Government) is a graduation requirement and that the grade they receive in this class will primarily be determined by choices they make during the year. In fact, I tell them that they should be able to tell me that first day what their final semester grade will be. I make it clear that their success or lack of success is primarily a matter of their own choices. "You know better than I do if you are going to do the work assigned and if you are going to put forth the effort to learn the material."

The first rule, underlined and bolded on the rule sheet, is that "in this room, everyone will be treated with respect." They value being respected themselves, but the business of their respecting others can be a problem. "Let me tell you what that will look like," I say. "When you are speaking, everyone in this room will be quiet and actively listen to what you have to say. On the other hand, when someone else is talking, you will be silent and actively listen to them. That's called respect."

The next part of the written class rules tells them in no uncertain terms that students are expected to come to school every day, to be on time, and to participate. "And let me define 'on time' to you. See that door? When the second bell rings, if you are on this side of it, you are on time, and if you are on the other side, you are late." It's a very binary thing. "And being late is not funny nor cute nor cool nor okay. Being late is *rude*. Every other person in the room got here on time, and your waltzing in here late is disruptive to the class and rude to them. And in this class, being rude has consequences— one hour of detention after school." Some of the students have been allowed to drift in whenever they chose to in every class for their entire school experience because it's a rule that takes energy from the teacher to enforce, and some teachers just don't. And the students who have always gotten away with being late have no intension of changing their ways. I pause here to emphasize that this will be a new day for them. Then I continue, "And yes, you will participate. You are here to actively participate in your own education. I am not here to entertain you.

There will be no heads on the desk. This is not nap time; it's school time."

Once you have established the class rules, remember that your new students have spent their lives with older people making up rules for them, and they will test you to see if you mean what you say or if it's just talk. We have all witnessed the mother in the store who tells her child time after time to stop doing something, and after four or five times, she stops saying anything and the child continues doing it. You must be tough, thorough, and fair in the enforcement of the rules. But if you do not intend to enforce the rules you make, don't make them. Making rules that you don't intend to enforce opens the door for problems you do not need. It makes you appear incapable of running the class.

A real danger in being a strict enforcer of rules is that students who do not like rules will not like the person/ teacher who enforces them. And over time, the things these disgruntled students can do against that teacher have increased. In my day, a child would never dream of confronting a teacher unless the teacher committed some egregious act. Today, students can go on to YouTube and watch a film appropriately titled "How to Get Your Teacher Fired." In short, the film advises that if the student wants to get their teacher fired, it's an easy process. The disgruntled child simply needs to make up some outrageous accusation against the teacher— the more vicious, the better—and take it to either their counselor, principal, or associate principal, and they will take it from there. According to YouTube, the best thing to do is to allege that the teacher "touched me." That will get every parent and administrator in their lives interested in preventing that teacher from continuing doing it. However, this charge can be defended against by the accused, demanding the time and place of the event, and if the teacher has been diligent in not being alone with any child, there will be witnesses that can refute the malicious charge. However, even if the teacher is relentlessly appropriate and there is no time that the teacher and the student were ever alone for the accusation to be possible, the film advises the accusing student to simply say that when they said or did something, "the teacher made me feel uncomfortable." That way, even if they were never alone with the teacher, the charge can be made, and the teacher can be accused of doing or saying something inappropriate. Not that anything they said was wrong or inaccurate, but that it made the student "feel uncomfortable," a charge that cannot be disproven.

All of us, in the course of talking about our subject or intending to begin a class discussion, have very likely made a statement supporting one side of an argument or the other or both, that some child somewhere in your classroom can take exception to. (Martin Luthor, the Monk?)

This kind of situation can and has been used to infer everything from racism to sexism on the part of teachers. Either of these accusations can be taken up by campus or community organizations, which can escalate the accusations, in defense of their children, to the school administration, even when the accusations are completely false. And these completely untrue accusations can be and have been used to demand that teachers be fired, just as the film counsels them. In short, teachers are public people, and when the adults around the child have trained them to seek out things to be offended by and have assured their child that the adults around them will not only support the child in their accusations, teachers or any public person can be accused of anything an angry young mind can dream up. The next step will be to escalate the accusation to the district that employs them and mark success in their mission only if they can damage or even end the teacher's career. If the adults can bring the accusation with enough determination and volume so that the ranking authority figures at the school or district are afraid of being sued by the community members for not taking adequate action, the principal and people at the district can find it easier to add credence to the false accusations made by the child by just acknowledging that what they say is possibly true than to stand up for the teacher, even if they have known and have observed their colleague for decades without ever having seen or heard anything that could support the accusation. A strong union, with specific contracted terms under which a union member can be fired, can be a godsend to a falsely accused teacher.

Teachers also have to remember that most children come to us experts at manipulating situations to their own benefit or to the disadvantage of others. And it is not only the strict teacher who can become victims of their anger or disrespect. One associate of mine was a young teacher who wanted to be the kids' friend and buddy, wanting the students to like him rather than take him seriously. He was above making rules, depending instead on his own youthfulness, personality, and the children's home-bred understanding of right and wrong behavior to operate the class. Within a few months, his classroom was out of control. "There were kids swinging from the light fixtures," according to one report, and of course, no education was happening. And like the evils in Pandora's Box, once disorder is loosed, order is hard to reestablish. The teacher, in this case, was forced to confront a frequent violator, a child taller and larger than he was who chose to challenge the teacher's authority, trying to dominate him using his sheer size, getting too close, and looming over the educator—a tactic that had likely worked for him his whole life. Eventually, the teacher had to push the child away, and that "push" and the student's subsequent and dramatic falling across a row of desks was the story that went home, spread to the outside world, and reported to the principal. The teacher was shocked and depressed by the personal affront to him and did not mount an adequate defense. He was subsequently transferred to another school as a disciplinary action.

In short, with a large flow of teenagers coming through our rooms, if there is going to be a rules structure (and there must be one), the teacher must establish it early and enforce it evenly and fairly. Most of all, when dealing with rules, you must be consistent. Even risking the possible wrath of a disgruntled student, it's important to be comparatively ogre-like at the beginning of the school year to establish expectations that have to do with each person, even the disrupters, being respected. If a student is rude or disrespectful, address it immediately. Remember how badly outnumbered you are. You must draw a line that the other students can see and appreciate. You can earn yourself the luxury of being your nice friendly self in April if you establish respect and insist on good manners in August. But always be alert. A single statement can be used against you, and they do not have to prove you did anything specific as in a court of law, only that you "made them feel uncomfortable."

And what do you do after you establish expectations? After that, the secret to classroom management is to keep the vast majority of your students' minds occupied doing things they consider in their own self-interest or at least kind of fun.

One day early in my teaching career, I asked my sister-in-law, "You have two bright and active boys. How do you keep them occupied and out of mischief?" She said that when she had her first son, she got the answer for how to keep him occupied and out of trouble from Grandma (her mother), who eventually raised five children of her own. "You have to keep their minds challenged. The bottom line is that children can concentrate on one thing or even on two things at a time and still have the ability to look around for something else to get into, but introducing a third thing for them to think about seems to occupy that remaining part of their mind, and they don't have the extra ability to look any further. When her children were in a store and causing a commotion, Grandma never yelled at them but would hold them and talk to them and pat them. In a moment, the child would calm down and not be "a problem." My sister-in-law translated that plan to "put a Tonka truck in one hand, a ball in the other, and tie a ribbon around their toe."

You cannot ever hold your students, nor should you ever pat them; however, you can assign them work to do. If students have something from yesterday to think about—perhaps using a quiz or warm-up exercise, something to do immediately today, and an assignment for tomorrow to begin planning for—it tends to keep them occupied. And usually, that's enough. Even when we are talking about the usually productive student, the beloved of God, the primary reason children of the "immediate satisfaction" generation who live their lives online to be troublesome is that they simply get bored. "You have to keep their minds occupied."

One way to keep our students today tuned in and in

a way they are accustomed to is to have them make use of their personal electronics to do their assignments. At my school, the vast majority of our students carry smart phones that they have become experts at using. Let's not fight the hopeless battle against the incursion of technology into our classrooms, but rather let's count this as prior knowledge and encourage them to be used. For an assignment, I have my students look up various pieces of data on their cell phones and then form a group to answer an analytic question about that data, such as which group of American Indian tribes would find it most difficult/least difficult to survive a winter during a given period of time? The group will then write and be scored on their ability to find data, analyze the data, and form an opinion and then write an essay supporting their answer. If this form of exercise is consistently done on Thursday, the sharper students may arrive having thought about it and with ideas as to how to do the assignment and then lead their group in that direction. (Remember, the idea is to have them thinking actively about what they are doing and what they may be doing tomorrow.) When classrooms are managed correctly, expectations are made clear, and the disrupters have not become the majority, the non-producers, disciplinary problems can be kept to a minimum. And the more creative the teacher can be in keeping their minds thinking about one, two, or three things, the more likely the students will remain occupied on task and enjoying the class. Remember, a Tonka truck in one hand, a ball in the other, and a ribbon around their toe.

CHAPTER 10

Q: What Kind of Support Can You Expect on Day 1?

A: Sink, swim, or learn to dance.

MY FIRST OFFICIAL ASSIGNMENT as a full-time teacher was in the business department, and I did have a degree in business and a teaching credential in that subject, but the actual work of the class itself was the Microsoft Office Suite (Word, PowerPoint, and Excel). This was long before every student on campus had many hundreds of dollars' worth of personal electronics in their pockets and when computers were still a cutting-edge high school graduation requirement. I had used most of the Office Suite programs in the course of my career, but not enough to teach them to someone else. As a result, for the first year, I had to get a copy of the textbook and reteach myself each chapter over the prior weekend, interpreting what the workbook directions meant and predicting the difficulties and questions the students might have before I spent the week teaching them. It went well, and I learned a lot about Office Suite and about teaching. It was my great good fortune that year to be paired up in that classroom with another teacher (Jim) who loved every aspect of technology. When the kids broke something, he fixed it. However, keeping my computer class functioning was my responsibility, yet one I was totally unsuited for. But that first year went well, and I really did enjoy the challenge.

For my second year, the administration moved me into a new classroom without my partner but with a new computer lab. The nightmare was that when they said "new computer lab," they really meant "future computer lab." When I opened the door for the first time, what I saw was a long table down the middle of the room, and on the table were broken keyboards, mouse controller, and other computer parts in piles about a foot high on the table. And I was expecting five classes of roughly thirty-five kids to show up the next week. What the heck?

When I asked members of the administration about the new computers, I was told, "We filled out the paperwork months ago for the new computers, but apparently, the district didn't process the order. No, we don't know when the computers will get here." The paperwork had been done and passed on to someone else, but it was no one's job to follow up. There was absolutely no sense of responsibility in the entire ordering process. Alas, we were not in the private sector anymore, Toto.

For the next three months, as I made daily calls to the district office, my students watched movies about people in the electronics world, such as Bill Gates, Steve Jobs, and Andy Grove, and I taught them to write papers about the movies. Now I have to smile to myself when one of my young colleagues tells me how badly his class is impacted when the repro room runs out of paper.

Being unsupported can also mean being unhindered by structure. These days, when I look back on my "sink or swim" time, I see a time when I was left alone to do my thing, to learn what works for me, and to create myself as an educator. I was free to invent and free to fail. Another common story among teachers is about their first day in front of their first class. After they have spent hours and hours "planning" their objectives and analyzing their delivery, after they have thought through every predictable aspect of their first class, "what will they say? What will I say?" They consider all the theories they learned about in teacher school classes. Anything that happens, they'll be ready for. And then, about ten minutes into their perfectly constructed lesson plan, they look around and notice that it is just not working for these kids. That is when you put on your dancing shoes and learn to be a teacher. You learn that you never really have a "class of thirty-five or so." What you have is thirty- five or so individuals, each of whom comes to your class with varying levels of interest in what you have to say. The teacher generally has a passion for the subject: history, English, Science, business, or a foreign language. They teach their subject because they love it. For most students, however, their attendance is a graduation requirement. Don't expect them to match your unbridled interest or your enthusiasm. And don't take it personally when they don't react as you hope they will.

CHAPTER 11

Q: What Do You Do about the Nonproductive Child?

A: Help them see that their current choices can lead to a desirable tomorrow.

JUST WHAT DOES "USEFUL and productive citizens" mean? First, we have to remember that students are people and not "units produced." Not once in all the years I was in the business of manufacturing did one of the units on the production floor refuse to be developed into a more useful, more well-developed form. To the chagrin of teachers, students do this all the time. They sometimes sit back as if to say, "Okay, I'm a child of the electronic age of instant information. Entertain me." Even in my classroom, where I will not allow students to sit and do nothing, and no parent would want me to, I have had up to an alarming 15 percent of my students recently who—no matter how many times I changed my methodology, tried to jazz it up for them, or have taken them outside to find out what the problem is, or no matter how many times I called or sent messages home to get the parents to help—simply refused to do what is assigned, maintaining a 15 to 35 percent F grade. After one such discussion with a young female student, she told me bluntly, "Mr. Murphy, no matter how much you push me, I'm going to do even less."

When nonproducing students are asked why a student as smart as they are is failing a class that should be easy for them to pass, their answer is almost universal: "I'm just lazy." And for all of their lives, people (their parents and teachers) have let the discussion end there. "Oh well," their teachers and parents have apparently said, "as long as they know there's a problem and that they have to fix it, I guess that's all I need to do." The students seem shocked when they are told that they are making choices that will likely bring horrible consequences to their futures. My conversation with them goes something like this:

"Do you ever want to move out of your parent's house and be independent?"

"Yes, of course," they said enthusiastically. "Do you expect that you'll need to get a job and make some money to move out and be independent?

"Yeah," they said markedly less enthusiastically.

"Well, what kind of job do you expect to get if you cannot even graduate from high school? Who do you think is out there looking to hire you? And how much money do you think you'll be making?"

Silence.

The very idea that they might not graduate from high school has never been a real possibility to them.

"Surely something will happen, and they will graduate— everyone graduates."

They know many people who did nothing in their classes, and all of those people graduated.

Then the follow-up questions:

"What kind of car do you want to drive, a piece of junk car that breaks down because that's all you can afford or a BMW, a Mustang, or other good cars?"

"A BMW."

"How in the world are you going to afford a good car like a BMW if you have to settle for a very low-paying job, even if you can find one?"

Additional silence and a final question: "And what

kind of girlfriend/boyfriend or spouse do you want to hang with, a good- looking and intelligent one or someone who themselves has to settle for someone who cannot even graduate from high school?"

Quiet. Sometimes a hint of tears...hopefully the beginning of a connection to reality. Wonder Woman has her golden lasso that makes people tell the truth, but I hope some of our upcoming educators will bring with them, along with their youth, something that connects with these children and allows them to hear the truth.

One of the best tools I have ever found to help kids turn around their academics is called a Flip-Flop Fo Sure.

Flip-Flop Buddies

After my two-year stint teaching computers, which included a large portion of time spent attempting to repair the machines that five classes of imaginative children could disable, and coming to the understanding that I am not the least bit technical, I knew it was time to transfer to the Social Studies Department and to teach history, economics, government, or other related subjects.

However, one does not simply transfer into another department that has achieved the delicate balance between its number of classes to be covered and the number of teachers currently in the department. The only way to transfer was to wait until there were more classes required than teachers available to teach them. Then and only then can a teacher from another department take on and teach that extra class. Over time, with a growing enrollment and teachers retiring, more classes can be added until the transfer is accomplished.

What is important to remember is that the teacher who takes that extra class is doing the associate principal a favor (it's their responsibility to cover that class), and you can use the situation to negotiate reassurances that if you take that class and others, the administration will promote and assist with your eventual transfer. (Think one hand washing the other.) As it happened, my first Social Studies class was made available because of the creation of a single uncovered World History section. I jumped at the opportunity, but beginning on the first meeting of the class, it became obvious that the students assigned to the class were *not* the ones classified as high-achieving. In fact, I believed at the time that the other World History teachers had been given a choice as to which students in their overcrowded classes should be transferred out to the newly created class. The result was thirty low-achieving students were matched with a teacher with limited teaching experience in that subject.

The kids, mostly tenth graders (but with a smattering of eleventh graders who had already failed the class), were adorable, including the two girls who were friends and always entered the room together, pretending to be airplanes, arms spread, complete with sound effects. But they had clearly never been taught any form of study skills, and before long, I was at my wits' end trying to get through to them, trying to help them achieve. I had soon spent the entire quiver of things I had learned in teacher school and in my time teaching computers, without much success.

One day, I must have raised my voice in frustration because after class was over and the children had all left, I heard a soft voice say, "Mr. Murphy." I looked up to see the kind smile and lovely blond hair of Mrs. Bernardini (Mrs. B), the teacher in the room next to mine. Apparently, I had been loud enough with my class to be heard through the flimsy room divider between our rooms. "Are you okay?" she asked softly. "We could hear you over here."

I apologized and attempted to explain my frustration. Mrs. B listened and offered a solution.

"Give them a Flip Flop Fo Sho," she said. "It will help, I guarantee it."

I had no idea what she was talking about, but I was willing to listen to any good idea.

"First," she said, "you go through the chapter you're teaching them and pick out twenty to twenty-five items that you want them to know, things that will *fo sho* be on the test. Then you teach them to fold up a useful prop to help them prepare for it themselves."

I was nodding, determined to understand. Mrs. B reached to pick up a piece of binder paper and folded it in half the long way, then folded each wing down again, leaving herself a piece of paper with four folded columns—two columns for data and two to use as cover-up flaps.

"The idea is for your students to use a tool that makes use of how their brains are actually wired." I was still watching, listening. She continued, "What is the emblem of McDonald's?" she asked.

"The golden arches," I replied. "Did you study that last night?"

"Of course not."

"Then how do you know?" "Because I see it all the time."

"Exactly. You see it all the time, and it registers in your memory. That's the way your brain is wired. How long is a television commercial?"

"Somewhere between fifteen and thirty seconds."

"Why do you think a multibillion-dollar industry like the advertising industry does that?"

"Because it works?"

"Exactly," she continued. "As your kids read through their chapter, have them fill out the definitions and other likely test answers from the chapter across from the items on your list. Then they should spend a few minutes flapping the flaps and quickly scanning the item you listed and whatever they wrote down from the chapter. And if they want it to work, they need to do this scanning as often as possible, at least three times every day. If they do it, they'll do great on the test, and their grades will improve. I guarantee it.

I've taught all my classes since and all my student teachers the benefits of the Flip- Flop Fo Sho, and it has always worked if the student is willing to actually do it. However, what does "doing it" mean? The answer is that after I make up my list of things that are *fo sho* going to be on the chapter test, the students are to fold up a piece of binder paper the same way Mrs. B had done that day. The list I give them is to be written in the second column, leaving room for notes between each entry. Then as they read through the chapter, when they come to that item, they are to ask themselves, "What question from the chapter is Mr. Murphy likely to ask about that?" and they write down facts that can answer that. I remind them that as juniors, they have been taking tests for eleven years and that they are just as capable of picking out good questions from the same reading as I am.

"And do not write down anything you already know. That would be a waste of your time and energy. For example, if the item I list is George Washington and you write 'a dude,' that's not wrong, but it's not likely to be asked on the test."

"Once you have completed your flip- flops, take about two to three minutes to scan the notes you've added. If you scan the list and your notes three times a day, every day, maybe when you're waiting for your ride home, or when your sister or brother has the remote control, taking about two to three minutes each time, when I give you the test, the answers will come to you, just like you know the emblem of McDonald's or Nike. If you do your flip-flops three times a day, every day, for about three minutes each time, you will do great on the test."

And it truly does work. The grades for my class soared, and the vast majority of my first social studies students passed the class.

As time went on, all the eventual new members of the Social Studies Department and I learned so much from Mrs. B that we came to think of her as the mentor of us all. However, what I learned most from my dealings with my flip-flop buddy is that sometimes education, whether as an individual or a school system, means having to stop doing what we feel comfortable with, what we have been trained to do, and changing to doing what works better for our students. In today's environment of uninterested students, frustrated teachers leaving education, and worsening environments inside schools, we need to understand that (like me) what the schools are doing is not working for the vast majority of our students. We need to rethink the very mission of our schools and examine doing things differently, maybe very differently.

CHAPTER 12

Q: How Important are Administrators?

A: Good administrators can make the whole process easier.

SCHOOL SOCIETIES CONSIST OF an odd number of principals, assistant principals, and other administrators; a couple thousand students; and a 110 or so teachers. Most administrators are former teachers themselves who have given up the classroom in search of more money or for the challenge of more widely or more effectively improving the educational system. Most are good, well-meaning people. I've been privileged to work with three sets of wonderful administrators. The problem is that I've worked with at least six sets of administrators. The good ones never stay as long as we would like, and the others stay far too long before being cycled out roughly every three or four years. Like any other supervisor or manager, good administrators seek out input from those with experience, who have reason to know, and lead by example, building communities and teams to advance what they see as best for the school and the students. Unfortunately, bad administrators, like bad supervisors or managers in industry, don't bother with any of those niceties and seem to believe and act as if their title or position instills power and wisdom on them and empowers them to give directives that are to be mindlessly followed. These unfortunates give unwise orders to long-term professionals that show little or no respect for their professional experience or for their input. One year, because our test scores had not reached our targets in the previous cycle, in November, one of our associate principals called in sets of three teachers at a time to personally order them to finish their entire year's curriculum (normally ending the last day of the semester in mid-June) by the date of the standardized test in mid-March. The logic being, if the material could possibly be on the test, we have to get to it by test day, even if we have to cram everything down the kids' throats. That meeting, being a precursor to disciplinary action, was clearly implied.

"Besides the fact that cramming seven months of curriculum into four months isn't enough time for the kids to take it all in, what should we do with them between mid-March and mid-June?"

"Have them do review projects or something." I promise that's what he said.

Of course, only a few of the most intimidated teachers given the directive did what he ordered them to do, and what effectiveness he had as an administrator on our campus ended abruptly.

At the same time, having good relationships with administrators can be very helpful, not only to the student teacher and the temporary or untenured teacher but to the tenured teacher as well. On a day-to-day basis, be it your teaching schedule, your access to scarce material, or even rapid room maintenance when the lights or the air conditioning malfunctions, it can be helpful to have a friend in the office.

The principal, him or herself, is very likely the person who will decide which of the various people on campus will get hired or not. If you are a student teacher at that school, be sure that your face and good reputation are known to the principal when the moment comes when he or she needs one more teacher in your department.

Oftentimes what happens is that the principal goes on with his day in late summer, thinking all is well. Then on or just before the opening day of school, because of unexpected increases in the number of students registering to attend, the principal comes under pressure to have a warm credentialed body in front of additional classrooms.

When that happens, make sure that he or she knows that you really want the job. Beforehand, it is important that you provide your mentor teacher with enough ammunition in the form of attitudes, professionalism, and skills you have demonstrated in their classroom to help them sing your praises in the office. Convince the principal that the school will be better off if you are working there and that letting you slip away would be a mistake. Make sure that the principal sees you as a solution to his late summer dilemma.

Once the new teacher gets hired, it will likely be an associate principal who will be assigned to perform their bi-annual evaluations. A longer period (two years or more) between evaluations is usual for a proven, more experienced teacher and perhaps shorter periods for beginning teachers. Either way, remember that the associate principal who evaluates you can be useful to your career if they become a big fan of yours. But you have to impress them. In a worst-case scenario, you can be dismissed for anything you do while you are probationary or for no reason at all. The administration can simply choose not to retain you. They can also put tenured teachers on a remediation track, which starts a two-year clock (or some other time period), during which if they don't improve to the administration's satisfaction, the teacher can be fired. Being tenured does not mean they can never be fired. It only means that experienced teachers cannot be dismissed without cause and that the administration must follow a remediation process, as is described in the union contract.

During a new teachers' evaluations, the administrator responsible for that evaluation needs to see them in control of their classroom and their curriculum. All students must be engaged, and the teacher must be actively moving about and encouraging them. This should be the teacher's typical classroom environment, anyway. It's essential that the evaluator see the teacher as a competent professional. And with all the years of training new teachers get in their subject matter and the classroom experience they've garnered during their student teaching and their career, each of them should have become a competent professional. New teachers should value the path they've taken and let it give them confidence. However, sometimes teachers at all levels of experience get worried when the subject of evaluation comes up. And in a perfect world, this should not be necessary. These teachers are in their classrooms every day delivering subject content, and the arrival of an administrator to observe them do it should make no difference. However, in a perfect world, the district office would not give observers the directive that "there should be more teachers on corrective action." Or, in a perfect world, no administrator would harbor a personal dislike for people they observe. As it is, some administrators/observers believe that they are obligated to find some major faults in every observation they make to simply justify their being in the room. In short, in a perfect world, workers, even workers with years of experience, many talents, and who do a fabulous job on a day-to-day basis, would not need a union to protect their rights from the abuse of power by management. Unfortunately, this is not a perfect world.

But to be clear, most administrators are good people who have a tough job, trying to manage a balance between competing and widely divergent and demanding constituencies, the teachers and others on campus, the district office that makes policy and can directly affect their individual careers, and the parents who can be both vocal and demanding in the interests of their children.

One apparent similarity between schools and a typical business model is that in both cases, those who receive product or services have unlimited demands and expect that if they can think of it and demand it effectively, those responsible for providing product or services should be expected to provide them, and to provide them immediately. Tasks are always easier to do, and the time required to accomplish those tasks is always less if you're not the one responsible to get them done. In schools, those who provide the services argue that they, without the respect or salary structure they deserve, have taken other people's surly and unmotivated children and for decades have been providing the educational basis of the most advanced technical civilization in the history of the world, only to be criticized because other countries with more homogenized, monolinguistic populations score higher on standardized tests.

The experiences supporting the following chapters on unions and evaluating schools were experienced in California. However, I've included them in this book for national publication because when it comes to social changes (think same-sex marriage and legalization of recreational marijuana), they tend to grow deep roots in California before flowering in other states and across the nation.

CHAPTER 13

Q: How Does the Union Help a Teacher?

A: The union contract provides a structure that ensures that management (the district and your local administrators) treat each employee in a consistent manner while also providing a method to adapt to changing circumstances.

FOR ALL OF MY previous working life, I had been a part of management, and I bristled at the choices presented to me on becoming a teacher. I had never been part of a union, but now I could either join the union, pay the fees and assessments, and be protected by the union and the contract, or I could choose to not join the union and forego that protection, but I would still have to pay the same amount of money in the form of a "service fee," which is defined as an amount "not to exceed dues, initiation fees, and general assessments." As most teachers do, I opted to join the union, and over the years, I have been happy to have joined the ranks of organized labor. However, let's not lose track of reality. The union contract is an agreement between two parties (the district and the union), and neither of them is the individual teacher. On the other hand, the teachers are a vital part of the discussion. No school district can function without teachers and their teaching credentials, and the union is just an empty structure if the teachers choose not to get involved in supporting their activities.

Article 1 of the contract (also referred to as "the agreement") establishes the parties to this agreement as the governing board of the district and the local union (East Side Teaching Association, in my case), which is associated with the California Teachers' Association (CTA) and then the National Education Association (NEA.) You, along with thousands of teachers in your union, are referred to in the agreement as a bargaining unit member.

The first goal of the district, as with any other management organization, is to efficiently get as much labor value out of its employees as is legal and will not cause a work disruption. The first goal of the union is to increase the number and organizational cohesion of its members with an eye to increasing their ongoing power and thus its bargaining position. Throughout these symbiotic relationships, it is quite possible that your personal interests and the interests of the union may differ. In my own case, I am a lifelong Republican, and every month, money is taken out of my check for use by the union in any way they wish. Over the years, this will amount to thousands of dollars, some of which my local union sends up to the national NEA, which in turn gives my money to their allies in the Democratic Party for political campaigns against the Republican Party. There have been a series of lawsuits filed around the country that have found their way to the Supreme Court to decide if this practice is illegal (source: 6-27-2018 EDSource.com, "High Court Ends Mandatory Fees Collected by Public Unions" by David Washburn and John Fensterwald). In 1977, the US Supreme Court set a precedent in the case of Abood v Detroit Board of Education, ruling that "unions could charge 'agency fees' as long as the proceeds were not spent on lobbying and political campaigns." In 2016, this finding was expected to be overturned in the case of Rebecca Friedrich v CTA but was deadlocked 4–4 when arch- conservative Justice Antonin Scalia unexpectantly died.

In 2018, the precedent set in Abood was overturned by a 5–4 majority in the case of Janus v American Federation of State County and Municipal Employees. Janus argued that the "fees" violated his First Amendment free speech rights (stating that he was forced to pay the fees, portions of which were donated to political parties, even though he disagreed with the union's political views). The union argued that the fees were not political speech; rather, they prevented "free riders" from benefitting from union work without paying for it.

Writing for the majority, Justice Alito said, "We conclude that mandatory fee requirements violate the free speech rights of non- members by compelling them to subsidize private speech on matters of substantial public concern." The result of this finding is that school districts and other public agencies are barred from deducting these fees from employees who have opted out of full union membership. Going forward, new employees must affirmatively agree to make any payments to the union *before* money can be taken from their paycheck.

What this all means in the life of a teacher is: every teacher knows of some case when a teacher has been falsely accused of some wrongdoing or runs afoul of some administrator who has a personal agenda. At these times, having a union representative stand up for them can be important to them continuing in their chosen career. This vulnerability can be enough to make the individual give up their free speech rights, and for very practical reasons, most teachers do just that.

The following is a summary of our union contract with the district concentrating on areas that may be of interest to new teachers or other stakeholders in the educational system. What is the relationship between the parties?

Article 2 recognizes the union as the exclusive representative of all certified employees, "except those positions for which an administrative credential is required," and that "work performed by the certified employees shall be performed by Bargaining Unit members, and shall not be subcontracted, supplanted or otherwise transferred out of the Bargaining Unit." But though the union is the only legal representative of teachers in the district, getting teachers to involve themselves in union activities can be a frustrating effort. When it comes to getting teachers to do disruptive union activities in the case of a dispute with management, union leaders are confronted with the fact that teachers are genuinely "nice," non-confrontational people and that getting them organized is like herding cats.

Both sides try to establish a mutually cooperative environment for future dealings with the other. Article 3 of the contract states that all employee organization activities will be conducted outside established classroom hours and will be conducted in neutral places. The agreement also establishes that the union, also known as the association, may use the district's e-mail, school mailboxes, and bulletin board spaces designated by the superintendent and that the district will furnish union representatives with the names, addresses, and phone numbers of the district's Bargaining Unit members. Most important to the union, the district agrees to provide the union with the name, address, date of hire, and work location of all newly hired teachers "no later than five (5) business days following acceptance of employment."

Article 4 warrants that "the exercise of the following powers, rights, authority, duties, and responsibilities by the district, such as the adoption of policies, rules, regulations, and practices…shall be limited by the specific and express terms of this agreement to the extent that such specific and express terms are in conformance with law."

Though Article 5 says that both the district and the association recognize the right of employees to form, join, and participate in lawful activities of the employee organization, and the equal alternative right of employees to refuse to form, join, and participate in or support employee association activities, the article continues to state that to remain employed as a teacher in the district, "each Bargaining Unit member shall maintain his/her membership in the association" and that any new bargaining unit member must "either join the association by executing a payroll deduction authorization for charges by the Union to be withheld or pay a "service fee not to exceed dues, initiation fees, and general assessments." And the district agrees to "promptly remit such monies to the association."

This article continues with the promise that the board shall not illegally discriminate against any bargaining unit member on the basis of any condition defined by law, such as race, color, creed, gender, national origin, political affiliation, marital status, age, disability, sexual orientation, membership in an employee organization.

Article 6 begins with the responsibilities of teachers when they need a sick day. "Whenever possible, a Bargaining Unit member must contact the District Substitute Service as soon as the need to be absent is known. Failure to provide adequate notice shall be grounds for denial of leave with pay or other disciplinary action, and stipulates that the District has the right to have the Bargaining Unit member examined by a physician designated by the District to assist in determining the length of time the member will be temporarily unable to perform assigned duties."

Article 6 continues by quoting the federal Family and Medical Leave Act, stating that eligible members are entitled to take unpaid leave for up to twelve (12) work weeks in a twelve-month period. The acceptable reasons for this leave will be the birth of a child (with an additional twelve weeks of bonding leave under CFRA), the adoption or initiation of foster care of a child, care for an immediate family member with serious health conditions, or the members own serious health condition. The member must provide thirty days advance notice when leave is "foreseeable" or as soon as possible.

But what happens when the member returns from a granted leave?

After a leave, the employee returning to work is "entitled to be restored to the same position of employment or an equivalent position with equivalent benefits, pay, and other conditions of employment." However, "personal necessity leave shall not be available solely for the purpose of personal convenience or for matters which can be taken care of outside work hours or for recreation activities."

What happens if a teacher needs to take sick leave or gets called for Jury duty?

Full-time bargaining unit members "shall be entitled to ten (10) days leave with full pay for each school year for purpose of personal illness or injury. Unused days will be accumulated by Bargaining Unit members for use during succeeding years." In addition, "any Bargaining Unit member called to jury duty or to appear as a witness in court may serve without loss of pay or other entitlement."

What if I need to take an extended leave sometime during my career?

"When approved, the Board shall pay Bargaining Unit members who are on a full years' leave 50% of their salary if they have 7 years of service to the District or 60% of their salary if they have 14 years of service to the District." Selection for leave approval will be made by the superintendent or designee solely on the educational need of the school with regard to the applicant's qualifications and record of service.

Can I request a transfer, or can I be transferred involuntarily?

The short answer is, yes, you can. Article 7 defines a transfer as a move from one full-time unit position to another at a different site. Bargaining unit members may apply for transfer by filing a transfer request form. Involuntary transfers "may be made when there is a need to reduce staff, or by the Superintendent when based on the legitimate educational-related needs of the District, and will not be arbitrary or capricious." Plus, "a Bargaining Unit member being transferred involuntarily shall be given the opportunity to express a preference for the destination school or position."

Involuntary transfers may be made by the superintendent or designee "when the school has need for the particular skills or competencies of the Bargaining Unit member." However, the agreement says that "no Bargaining Unit member shall be involuntarily transferred outside their credential area."

A full-time bargaining unit member who requests a transfer for two (2) consecutive years and does not have the transfer granted "shall be guaranteed a transfer upon their third consecutive request." However, this guarantee shall be dependent upon the existence of an open position for which the Bargaining Unit member is "credentialed and qualified." Even then, the member is only guaranteed a position, not a specific site or assignment. And if a position is offered and rejected, the member loses primary transfer rights.

A bargaining unit member who has been served with a notice of unprofessional conduct or incompetence or where the most recent evaluation has been unsatisfactory or where the member is currently in a remediation program shall not be eligible for transfer under this section.

What rights does an employee have if they are assigned to workdays that are split between two sites?

Split assignments are when "a member normally assigned to one school shall be split between sites." This member shall teach no more than four periods in a school day unless agreed to between the administration and the member. Members with split assignments will have a travel period as a part of their working day, and if a member agrees to teach a fifth period, they will be paid for the extra period taught.

Both parties to the agreement agree in article 9 that during layoffs, the district will honor seniority as required in Education Code 44955 and that bargaining unit members who are reassigned or transferred as a result of a reduction in force for a particular position or department "will have the right of first refusal to such positions as they are restored" and the "first criterion for ranking rights of members to a restored position shall be years of District service in that position or department."

Article 10 talks about summer school, beginning with "summer school must be authorized by the Board of Trustees" and that "Bargaining Unit members will be notified of available employment no later than five (5) working days after the Board of Trustees has authorized the summer session. Qualified Bargaining Unit members will be given preference in hiring over other applicants. However, though selected, the Bargaining Unit member will only be used if class enrollment continues to meet District standards." In addition, "summer school teaching assignments shall be filled for a particular site by applicants from that site first," and if there are more applicants at a particular site than there are positions, "seniority, prior participation in such special programs, and special training will be considered for placement." At the same time, a bargaining unit member who designs a particular course to be taught during summer school will be offered first priority during the summer of introduction only, provided that the teacher's credential(s) authorizes services in the area of the course." A bargaining unit member who recruits students to the extent necessary to meet district's requirements "will be offered the first priority appointments for the introduction year only, provided the teacher has the appropriate credentials."

How are teachers evaluated?

It depends on that teacher's employee status. Article 11 begins with the edict that "every temporary teacher hired before the second semester shall be evaluated once during the school year," and that "every probationary teacher shall be evaluated by the administration at least once every school year, not later than the end of the first semester." In each of these cases, "a conference and written summary evaluation letter shall be completed not later than ten (10) working days after the evaluation of the teacher, unless mutually agreed upon."

At the same time, the agreement states that "every permanent teacher with fewer than ten (10) years of employment with the District will be evaluated not less than every other year" and that "a unit member with permanent status who has been employed at least ten (10) years with the District" and is highly qualified as defined in 20 USC 7801 (ESEA) and whose previous evaluation rated the employee as "meeting or exceeding standards," and if at that time the evaluator of record placed the unit member off track, shall be evaluated every five years if the unit member and the evaluator consent. "However, either party may withdraw consent after the first off track year with written notice no later than the fifth working day of the school year in which the Bargaining Unit member will be evaluated. The Superintendent or designee will consult with the Association President or designee with respect to and prior to the withdrawal of consent."

At any rate, every permanent teacher who is not on remediation or on the Unsatisfactory evaluation track shall be notified in writing of his/her status as on track or off track by September 15 of any given year. If on track, such notification shall identify the teacher's Administrator of Record and will contain the self-evaluation profile for completion by the on-track bargaining unit member and will be returned to the Administrator of Record no later than September 30 of any given year.

Before November 1, any permanent teacher who is on track may request of the principal/director that the Administrator of Record be changed. Should the principal/ director agree that the change of evaluator is warranted, such change will be made before any formal work on the evaluation begins. If the Administrator of Record is not changed, the permanent teacher can appeal the decision to the Director of Human Resources.

To begin the evaluation process for permanent employees, the evaluator shall schedule pre-evaluation "intake interviews" with on-track permanent teachers, during which the parties will choose between a nontraditional observation (where a teacher may work as an individual or as a member of a team to complete a project reasonably related to his or her subject area and expertise). This may be project- based, portfolio-based, experiment-based, or performance-based. However, should a permanent teacher be unable to complete the non-traditional evaluation, the default process will be a traditional evaluation, which consists of a pre-observation conference, the observation itself, and a post-observation conference. At the pre-observation conference, the Administrator of Record and the teacher "shall mutually agree to the elements upon which the evaluation is to be based, based upon the California Standards for the Teaching Profession, and include Objectives set for the specific lesson to be observed, the means of assessing whether these objectives were met, and a review of how this lesson fits into the over-all curriculum." The bargaining unit member and the evaluator are required to make a good faith attempt to reach mutual agreement on the member's goals and objectives, but if they disagree, the evaluator shall state reasonable goals and objectives by which the member is to be evaluated. "The Bargaining Unit member may specify his/her positions, in writing, to be attached to the evaluation documents, including any constraints which the member believes inhibit his/ her ability to meet the stated goals and objectives." Any dispute of the reasonableness of the goals and objectives may be grieved between the bargaining unit and the district.

The evaluator will notify the on-track bargaining unit member of the date and period when the formal observation will take place. And a summary letter shall be submitted to the bargaining unit member no more than ten (10) working days after the formal observation unless an extension is mutually agreed to on the Evaluation Option Plan. Upon receiving the formal observation letter, the unit member will sign and date it, acknowledging only their receipt of the document, not that they particularly agree with it. The unit member will be provided the opportunity to attach a written response that shall become part of the permanent record. "An exit interview will occur for each on track permanent employee not later than April 30 of the evaluation year unless agreed to in writing on the Evaluation Option Plan." At the exit interview, bargaining unit members must be told of their status for the following year: off track, on track, on remediation, or Unsatisfactory track. If the unit member has been employed at least ten (10) years with the district and is "highly qualified" and whose previous evaluation rated the employee as "meets or exceeding standards," his or her status for four (4) years will be off track, with the fifth year designated as on track.

To put a permanent employee on the remediation track, the employee must have been on track immediately prior to being placed on remediation. "Prior to this action, the Administrator of Record must observe the permanent teacher at least two (2) times in the first semester, then observe the permanent teacher at least three (3) times in the second semester (All second semester observations must be completed by April 15, and at the conclusion of each observation, within five (5) working days, a written communication, identifying the weaknesses and recommendations for correction of these weaknesses, shall be sent to the permanent teacher." And a formal evaluation must be completed in each semester prior to the permanent teacher being placed on remediation. The second formal evaluation must be completed by April 15 but not before March 1, after the second semester observations have been completed, and the second summary letter (completed within five (5) working days of the formal evaluation) shall identify the permanent teacher's performance as "Unsatisfactory" or "Needing Improvement." At the exit interview, the bargaining unit member shall be notified of his/her status for the following year as "On Remediation."

During the remediation year, "a Remediation Plan must be completed by the Administrator of Record and the permanent teacher must be notified of the Plan no later than the fifth (5) working day of the school year." The Administrator of Record will attempt to meet and share the Remediation Plan in person; however, should the bargaining unit member be unavailable, the Remediation Plan shall be mailed by registered mail to the last residence mailing address the site administration has for the member, post marked no later than the fifth working day of the school year.

As part of their employment continuance, permanent teachers who are on remediation are required to participate in an assistance program, which will be provided by the district, where exemplary teachers will assist the teachers on remediation in the areas of subject matter knowledge, strategies, classroom management, as well as teaching methodologies whenever appropriate. And the agreement stipulates that these sessions are to be "supportive in nature and in no way evaluative."

A permanent teacher who has successfully completed a year of remediation is then placed on track for the next school year. A permanent teacher who has been partially successful during his or her remediation year shall be placed on remediation for the next year. And a permanent teacher who has been unsuccessful during the remediation year shall be placed on the Unsatisfactory evaluation track. The name and evaluation record of permanent teachers being placed on the Unsatisfactory track shall be sent to the Board of Trustees who will "approve the concerted effort of the site and District Administrations to either remediate or dismiss the permanent teacher placed on the Unsatisfactory track, which may end their career. At any point, the Bargaining Unit member who shows a good faith effort at correcting the deficiencies may be removed from the unsatisfactory track and placed on Remediation." Approval for this change will be at the discretion of the district.

What does the contract say about my workday?

The final articles of the contract state that "the number of scheduled work days for Bargaining unit members shall be one hundred and eighty-two (182)" with exceptions being made for certain nonteaching positions. And "the Bargaining Unit member's regular workday is seven (7) hours, exclusive of a duty-free lunch." In addition, the agreement stipulates that "a Bargaining Unit members workday begins fifteen (15) minutes before the Unit members first assigned periods and ends 7.5 hours later, which includes at least fifteen (15) minutes after the Unit members last assigned period. And in no event shall a Bargaining Unit member's workday exceed seven (7) hours exclusive of a duty-free lunch." However, the agreement also states that "full-time Bargaining Unit members shall participate in other duties for a maximum total of twenty-five (25) hours, which shall include, but not to be limited to: activities supervision, mandatory back-to-school night, site and District meetings, department meetings, IEP meetings which cannot be scheduled during the workday and other assignments consistent with the Education Code and the policies and regulations of the District."

In addition, "all full-time bargaining Unit members for whom the school principal is the immediate supervisor shall have a preparation period, which is intended to be used for professional purposes which may include but not limited to the preparation of lessons, meetings with students, or carrying out other duties as assigned by the principal or designee when the need arises."

And payment at the resident substitute rate will be paid to the bargaining unit member who are assigned to supervise students during their preparation period.

Finally, how much will I get paid?

The District Certified Salary Schedule is posted as part of Appendix A of the agreement and is a public record available to everyone. The salary schedule is organized with four columns, reflecting semester units of education the employee has earned after a bachelor's degree. The first column of the schedule reflects payment with just a BA, the second column reflects the amount paid with the advancement of thirty (30) semester units beyond a BA, and the third column reflects the amount paid with the advancement of a BA plus forty-five (45) semester units. To get to the fourth and final column requires obtaining sixty semester units after a BA with or without the inclusion of a master's degree.

Once an employee finds their appropriate column, the other determinant is years of experience and service. As time goes by, the teacher's salary rises. This structure rewards educators who continue their education after becoming teachers. Simply put, if you earn more units after your bachelor's degree, you make more money. I didn't and I don't think any non-teacher truly understands why teachers need to take off nearly three months in the summer. Now I do. Spending seven hours a day every day teaching kids is exhausting. Teachers need the time off to regain some semblance of physical and mental well-being.

One thing that has always made me wonder is when a teacher feels they have to teach summer school "because I need the money." What they don't understand is that if they spend their summers earning extra semester units, their salary can rise high enough that they do not need to teach summer school. The best part is that they only have to earn the extra semester units once, and the extra money comes in as long as they work there.

When I made the change from private industry to teaching, I knew that my salary would be less than it had been, but I didn't know how much less. I was determined that I wanted to be a teacher, and that was that. Finally, after all my paperwork was done and I was hired, I asked the Human Resources lady how much I would be making. Respecting privacy rules, she quietly wrote down and passed me the slip of paper. I looked at the number and asked her, "A week?" She smiled, shook her head, and whispered, "A month." In the end, the union and its contract does provide a teacher/ bargaining unit member with a degree of security that allows them to both function on a day-to-day basis but also the flexibility to evolve.

CHAPTER 14

Q: How Does the State Evaluate the Schools Themselves?

A: The evaluation process is evolving.

THINGS ARE CHANGING DRAMATICALLY in our state and in most other states, but what happened historically when it came to evaluating our public schools was that in the spring of each year, the state mandated that standardized tests be given to all students in appropriate grades to demonstrate that our students had retained the data contained in the curriculum appropriate to their grade. The question being, of the important things included in the state- mandated standards, what did the students remember on the day of the test?

For the teacher, this meant lessons based on scaffolding (structuring new data on and through a bedrock of the child's prior knowledge) and repetition. Once taken, each child's test was sent out of state, where it was scored, and some months later (after the summer break and during the following semester), the scores were reported back to the school. Since they had to take these tests almost every year, the students knew that the tests were scored by someone somewhere off campus and that the results of each year's testing were not coming back until the following school year, in the fall, after they had moved on to a whole new schedule of classes and a list of new teachers who did not use the resulting test scores in calculating current grades. In short, there was neither an immediate incentive for them to do well nor any form of consequence for them doing poorly.

Beyond scoring each student individually, using the test results, the schools were also evaluated on how well they addressed the success gap between social groups. What this meant is that not only did these out-of-state entities evaluate the performance of the school using the individual student's tests but that the school was also evaluated on the basis of the child's racial and economic circumstances by subgroup. Ours, being a public high school, was responsible to achieve state-mandated improvement goals for all grades and for all subgroups. Scoring well in total was not enough. Each significant subgroup (measured by the percentage of the student population represented) was required to meet the state-described minimum growth goal as well. And there were "scare them" stories spread around about other schools and other school districts which had failed to meet the state-mandated growth goals for one or more of their sub-groups (for two or more years) and were first labeled "Performance Improvement" schools or districts (a warning). And then, if noticeable improvement is not seen, they were "taken over by a state administrator who cancelled the union contract and took away all of their benefits."

This threat tended to motivate the administration and the teachers but not so the children actually taking the exams. And except for admonishing their students to do well because it's "the right thing to do" or "you should do your best for your school," teachers and the administrators, in practice, could do scant little to entice their students to perform their best if they didn't choose to. The test results, and as such the evaluation of the work the school and staff were doing, were literally in the hands of the children, with whatever motivation they may have brought with them that day. Many students felt that forced tests that did not immediately affect them were an imposition and a waste of their time. In short, it was the perfect time to protest, or to use 1960's jargon, a chance to "stick it to the man." (Where do you think they got that?)

The immediate cure for the timing delay in reporting the outcomes should have been to publicize successful students and make the annual testing a component part of their current grade for the current semester. We should have cut through the testing bureaucracy and made the student taking the test at least share the accountability for the outcome. In the age of immediate information, the tests should have been scored immediately, assigned a given weight and percentage of the current semester's grade, with the students knowing that if they did do well, there were rewards or consequences if they did not. Without this sense of accountability, the test results were meaningless as a way of evaluating either the schools or the teachers. And that is why teachers balked at having their wages pegged to student test scores.

As it was, the following year, when the scores came back in, whether the school had done well but wanted to do even better or did not achieve its goal scores, the administrators identified which socioeconomic groups did well and which did not. Then in a meeting with the total school staff, we "brainstormed" how we, as a school, would bring up the scores of those "underperforming" subgroups. Identifying these subgroups, though, was easier than solving the problem of "underperforming." For one thing, when would identifying the nonperforming student subgroups and then forming and enforcing a remedial plan be seen as racial profiling?

Under the threat of getting low scores and being branded as a "Performance Improvement" district (and being taken over) on the one hand and possibly being sued for institutional racism on the other, over the years, our school delicately walked the line, identifying which groups were which and then quietly creating programs to support the underperformers. Then attempting to broaden their methods to be even more inclusive of all students at all levels, the teachers created lesson plans and organized activities with the underperforming groups in mind, and the administration created new outreach programs, empowered minority parent groups on campus, and made home contacts with the families and the local community seeking out ways to improve student performance. Yet over the years, the underperforming subgroups tended to remain the same ones, and their testing levels remained subpar.

Each year there were episodic improvements, but for some of our families and for some members of our school community, too many of the students we were teaching (and finding some way to have them pass our classes, only to have them do poorly year after year on the standardized tests) had to then translate and explain the situation and what it all meant to their parents, some of whom desperately wanted their children to succeed and be educated. Yet again, for some students taking the test, demonstrating their success in school is not only contrary to their personal goal; it stands in direct contrast to their family's expectation of them. Yet, the schools and the school districts were evaluated using tests given to students who put into the process as much or as little as they chose to that day. As it eventually happened, the tests themselves were done away with. We are currently replacing the historical standard tests with a new version more aligned with the Common Core, emphasizing more evaluation and data usage and less data recall. It is yet unclear if the problem of lack of reward or consequences will persist.

The bad public image of the public schools gets worse and comes under increased scrutiny every time a report comes out revealing that American students have come up short again compared to students around the world on standardized tests. (The use of the term *standardized* implies that each student has an equal chance to show their proficiency. The message the testing process sends is that given that all children are created equal, and if anything, perhaps American kids should be expected to be a little extra equal.) The difference between the students' performance on a yearly test can be equated to the quality of the schools they attend and the instruction they receive there). The American taxpayers and parents are appalled at their students' comparatively low achievement ratings because they know they spend billions of dollars every year on education, only to come out ranked somewhere around twenty-seventh in the world. Scandinavian or Asian countries come in on top, and our students score somewhere behind Uganda or Senegal.

We find all of this unacceptable, to say the least, and a national humiliation, to be more brutal. So what is the solution? Is our system broken? How do we fix it? Of course, we begin by identifying the problem. In America, we expect and demand that our investments give us identifiable and appropriate returns. In addition, as children of the Industrial Revolution, we believe that problems in a system can be evaluated and corrected as needed. That's why likening education to a factory model, a business model is our natural response. By using a business model, we seek to avoid emotions, identify the problems in the system, and then make needed corrections. The problem in American education, therefore, should be solved by analyzing it systematically. We give them our money; we should hold the schools accountable. Few would disagree. The problem in "politically correct" America is that the solution to the problem has to be *acceptable* as compared to *true*.

But a business model?

Schools are a microcosm of society with layers of variables that we did not have to deal with in industry. We made our money from developing, processing, and shipping a product that met customer specifications. Critics might say, "Your industry was judged and had to struggle to survive by the value to society of what you produced. Why should schools be any different? Society sends the schools free raw material in the form of students, we pay all your expenses, the business of the school is to educate them (which they have done for hundreds of years and should be a well-honed process, yes?), and to graduate/ship them into society, meeting the specifications demanded by the customers, hopefully in the case of schools as useful and productive citizens."

Again, what does "useful and productive citizens" mean? Historically, the public school system was established to assimilate immigrant children into society and make them more "American." Millions of people have come to America from all over the world and have made this country the "exceptional" country of the world that it is. No matter where our families originated, no matter where they rank on a "hierarchy of oppression," it would likely have been easier and less frightening for our forefathers and foremothers to remain there, to stay put. But someone in almost every American's gene pool acted incredibly bravely and decided to leave where they were, sometimes risking their lives along the way, in order to make a better life here. Even, perhaps especially, if the ancestor was brought here involuntarily as a slave, all the groups that now make up the American "salad" have had to struggle to survive and to prosper when they got here, and have ever since. Being an American is not and never has been easy. Depending on exactly when or how they became part of the teaming mass, the society our ancestors were becoming part of was in some phase of industrialization, meaning that to advance in their new world, they had to learn to speak, read, and write in acceptable English and to do minimal arithmetic. Barred from interference by the federal government by the ideals of the reserve clause of the Tenth Amendment, private and eventually state schools served this purpose for decades. However, this was before the social shock of World War II that ended with a constant fear between the American West and the allies of the Soviet Union.

When the Soviet Union launched their Sputnik satellite in 1957, it was the early Cold War, and we in America and the West did not know how to do satellites. When the Reds successfully launched their satellite, "We the People" freaked out, and Congress created the National Aeronautics and Space Administration (NASA) to advance and to oversee research in rocket science and space exploration. Congress also passed the National Defense Education Act, getting the government more deeply involved in education. Sputnik represented a level of technology in the hands of a sworn enemy that was beyond us, and we reacted by requiring our children/

students to take higher math and science classes, hopefully leading the next generation to become scientists and engineers, to keep us up with the Soviets. It was the arms race and the space race, and this meant that everyone with half of an aptitude for education had to go to college. It was an educational Pearl Harbor. We needed every good mind we could get. Our nation was in danger. We needed to get our inventive muscles flexing. And it worked. We invented everything from Velcro to Tang to space travel to the microprocessor. It worked, and we felt great. We actually did land a man on the moon and brought him back safely. America was ahead again, the undisputed technological leader of the world. But when the threat of Soviet domination of space was over, we saw economic competition with other countries and commerce itself as reasons to keep the increased science and math requirements in place in our schools and to actually expand them. What this continued emphasis on increasing technology and limited school budgets did was to eventually crowd out competing subjects like art, wood shop, music, electronics, welding, auto shop, home economics, and most other elective classes— many of which the students actually found useful and were genuinely interested in. It was a space through which students not interested in college could move through and actually learn useable life skills.

In addition, the ensuing 1960s changed our thinking about other things. At one time, morality and personal ethics were taught at home or in churches. These were the responsibility of parents and the home. Parents knew that the teachers were extensions of themselves, both working for the betterment of the children. And they supported each other, or as my father once told me, "If you get into trouble at school, you'll be in bigger trouble when you get home." This cut through some of the nonsense and focused us on the learning we had come to school to do.

Another difference between schools and the "normal" business environment is that if someone in the business world chooses not to do what they are asked to do by those in positions of responsibility, they get fired, sent away, and replaced by someone who wants to do the job. The supervisor or manager doesn't fire people who don't perform because they're bad people but because they must also do as they are directed, achieve prescribed goals, or face dismissal themselves. This process rewards performance and accountability, not reluctance. This changes the entire atmosphere and motivates people.

Firing them (failing them) and sending them away for

nonperformance are still not acceptable consequences that schools are allowed to make use of except when dealing with the most egregiously nonperforming students.

The best hope for success we have today is to make our schools serve the purpose of preparing our children for life after twelfth grade to fully institute some version of the Common Core standards (including the school to work component) and then use the WASC accreditation process to enforce it.

(More on Common Core, WASC, and the creation of educational convoys later.)

CHAPTER 15

Q: What Have We Tried So Far to Improve
   Our Schools?
A: If it looks like it will help, teachers are
   willing to give it a try.

THE PEOPLE WHO MAKE up our educational system genuinely feel responsible for each child under their care and want their students to excel in life. In fact, for at least the past twenty years, due to the societal perception that the schools should be performing better as demonstrated by international standardized tests or because of an American malaise on the subject of education in general, people at various higher levels in the education establishment have periodically felt it necessary to at least look like they're doing something to address the problem by creating and implementing some "enlightened" new program at their local schools. Our experience has been that these people tend to stay in positions for only a few years before collecting their comparatively large paychecks and moving on, knowing that both the attempt and any success achieved with their new program will look great on their resumé for their next position. The result is that every four to five years, a new program gets instituted on the local level in the hope that the students will perform better, not based on the idea that problems in the schools are manifestations of problems of society mixed with the personal expectations and goals of children and their parents but based on the fallacy that "if the schools just delivered the content better or in a different format, the students, as measured by standardized tests, will feel better motivated and then perform better."

My first experience with this process was called block scheduling, where the thinking was that if we changed from breaking up the day into five or six classes lasting fifty-five minutes, five times a week, and switched instead to rotating ninety-minute-to two-hour classes, perhaps twice or three times a week, we could cut out an amount of passing time spent between classes, allowing each teacher to spend more quality time with each student. And that would be good. Most of my fellow teachers and I at the time jumped at the opportunity. We would have to recreate our lesson plans for the longer, less frequent schedule, but if the new schedule had any chance of improving things for our students, we were for it.

"C'mon, it could be great. Let's do it."

We had time allocated for "professional development," and we spent hours discussing best practices and preparing for the implementation. Then problems arose, chief among them the "fact" that block scheduling made scheduling classes for 2,400 students more complicated, which delayed implementation till the following year. We also went through personnel changes during the ensuing year, and some of the leading proponents of block scheduling moved out of their positions, and the idea was postponed another year, by which time people just lost interest, and the program at our school was shelved permanently.

The next idea to come around was called Schools within Schools, where, beginning with the incoming freshman and sophomore classes, each student would be assigned to a small cadre, all of whom would have the same limited number of teachers as they progressed through their day. The thinking here was that if these students all had the same teachers, with the same assignments and in-class practices, an air of small-town commonality would grow and nurture the students to higher achievement. However, to schedule that many students into small bands became even more difficult than it was with block scheduling, and Schools within Schools was likewise abandoned.

A few years later, another idea came into vogue. "Let's hire an education consulting company, pay them bundles of money, and they can tell us how to do our teaching better." And so we did. But the criticism of consultants in the business world is that they come into your place of business and borrow your watch to tell you what time it is. Once again, many of us optimistically met with the consultants, told them everything we knew about teaching and what we hoped for, only to have their recommendations sound like what we already knew, and programs to implement the consultant's findings were found to be difficult, not as productive as at first hoped, and ultimately also abandoned.

It's important to note that by just taking notice of our statistical shortcoming and our aggressively positive reactions to them have brought about a gradual uptick in our school's statistical performance (we moved from rating fourth in our twelve-school district to third), so we remain encouraged and willing to experiment.

Though not totally new, another idea has come into vogue. Let's eliminate grades all together. According to an article in *the San Jose Mercury News* (by education writer Sharon Noguchi, 09-17-17), more than 120 elite private high schools have begun a movement to eliminate grades and GPAs from schools. According to Than Haley, the head of Menlo School, a private college prep school located in affluent Atherton, California, "75% of students in his school have a 4.0 average, making grades meaningless." The overriding argument against awarding students who perform well higher grades is that "students focus more on grades than on education." Another stated goal of the movement is to avoid adolescent stress. Healy adds that "the (San Francisco) Bay area is ground zero in stress and anxiety among students" and that the time has come for a national conversation. The answer, according to Menlo and other elite private schools, is to "dump grades" and create a "digital annotated transcript that might reflect more than a student's mastery of topics in math, science, and reading." The improved transcript would also measure such areas as academic growth, collaboration, entrepreneurship, empathy, honesty, and creativity. According to proponents, "each transcript would be linked to a homepage containing samples of the student's actual work and achievements." Another group of proponents, the Mastery Transcript Consortium, offers to construct and bring to agreement a replacement for the five-letter grading system that was "invented 123 years ago at Holyoke College in Massachusetts" and to do it in five to seven years.

Another proponent of a system without grades, Sal Khan (founder and CEO of Khan Academy, whose Khan Lab School is a member of the Consortium), notes that "the problem with grades is that they are wildly inconsistent from one classroom to another." In addition, Khan adds that grades reinforce a "fixed mindset" within the individual student as either a C student or an A student or in between. Then "having been labeled subpar, the student checks out." Khan continues that "the goal is to help them master content without judging them." Khan would like to replace the current education system that dictates progression through grades by age with one that shows students achieving proficiency as they advance.

Consortium members believe that grades create a toxic hyper- competition among students who believe that only straight A's will get them accepted to the college of their choice. One question, of course, is: can the more textured multilayered evaluation embraced and proposed by these private schools, with average class sizes of 14 and an average teacher load of 4 classes, be manageable for public school teachers with an average of 175 students in 5 classes?

Following the "law" that says, "Anything seems possible to those who don't have to do it," Khan thinks it's possible by involving peer reviews and electronic feedback. He says, "The tools are available to make mastery learning and evaluation practical."

In his article, "The Case against Grades" on Slate.com, educational writer Michael Thomson asserts that "the structure of grading students is the biggest culprit in America's long steady decline in education."

The current grade-oriented system is the reason that SAT Reading results are at a forty-year low, and according to Thompson, "the rigid and judgmental foundation of modern education is the origin point of many of our worst qualities, making it harder for many to learn because of its negative reinforcement."

How did the current system of grades come to dominate education? Children had historically been trained at home to do helpful tasks around the family farm and normally evaluated by their parents. As early as 1792, hoping to inject objectivity to their training, William Farish, a chemistry professor at Cambridge, first advocated evaluating children's performance using qualifying test results. By 1897, Farish's system of testing had been transformed into a letter-based scale at Mount Holyoke College in Massachusetts and was then adopted by a wide group of schools and Universities around the country. The acceptance of a letter grading system coincided with the rapid expansion of legally compulsory education in America, finally being adopted by all states by 1917. Grades became the foundation of that expansion.

Modern critics of today's process argue that "fear of negative outcomes is a major impediment to learning." It is, they contend, the fear of a negative outcome that causes the "classic symptoms of procrastination, confusion, and lower self-esteem, leading to disengagement." Critics also claim that "willingness to take on challenging tasks diminishes when grades are involved." John Taylor Gatto, a teacher turned fierce education critic, has proposed an educational system based on "independent study, community service, a wide variety of experiences, privacy and solitude, and a thousand different apprenticeships."

The most famous example of Mr. Gatto's proposed system, the Montessori schools, are noted for their lack of grades, multiage classes, and students choosing their own projects from a selected range of materials. A 2006 comparison of Montessori and grade-based students found that Montessori students "performed better than grade-based students at reading and math," and they "wrote more creative essays with more complex sentence structures, selected more positive responses to social demands, and reported feeling more of a sense of community in their school."

What is proposed instead of today's educational experience is a classroom without pedagogy and rank, without motivating students, teachers, and underperformers with the fear of being flunked, fired, or shut down, a system that would form a child's education around his or her eagerness to discover, contribute, and share.

As long as there have been schools, especially publicly funded schools, there have been people imagining how to do the job better. Fortunately, or not, most dream scenarios are filtered out by what turns out to be practical at the time or made to wait for future acceptance. Our current system, grades and all, has its shortcomings and its critics; however, eliminating grades seems an idea whose time has not yet come. First of all, if 75 percent of a school's students have 4.0 averages, the major problem at that school is a bad case of grade inflation, indicating a lack of rigor in their curriculum. The only place I know of where "all the children are above average" is Garrison Keeler's fictional Lake Woebegone. Secondly, generally speaking, grades do not create dangerous levels of stress in students. In fact, stress can be a great motivator. Grades, if given fairly and objectively, are simply indicators as to how a student is performing against a certain teacher's curriculum and expectations. Extreme stress occurs when the student or their parents have set acceptable minimal expectations that are higher than the limits the student can or chooses to perform at. Indications or reports that students are under stress is not a reason to eliminate the evaluation and reporting process but are an indication that expectations and results are out of alignment. It's more complicated than just saying the grade system is bad; parents and students have to manage expectations versus accomplishments. Then there's the argument that grades are not consistent classroom to classroom. It's a fact: they are not exactly consistent. Just as no two ministers will deliver their sermon the same and no two doctors will have the same bedside manner, no two teachers will perform their tasks (covering material, assigning, or evaluating) the same either. In a student's future, their boss, their customers, or some number of people in their work environment will evaluate them, and no two evaluation processes will be exactly like the others. It is not being graded, which causes stress in children. Children stress when there are differences between the grades they earn and the expectations they or their parents have set for them.

One idea mentioned: that students and a cadre of other stakeholders in their lives should work together to provide each student the most interesting, expansive, and challenging experience that they can create in the child's education, experiences that prepare them step by step (elementary schools that prepare them for middle school, middle schools that prepare them for high school, and high schools that prepare them for either college or the world of work) to be responsible members of the society they will one day be a part of. Or, as Mr. Khan says, a system that "shows students achieving proficiency as they advance." (See "educational convoys" in chapters 16 and 18.)

CHAPTER 16

Q: Can the Common Core Be an Answer?

A: If we commit to goals and invest resources, the Common Core could lead the way to a better future.

ONE OF THE NEWEST big things and perhaps the potentially most beneficial idea in education today is a mix of the Common Core State Standards (CCSS), along with, to a limited extent, the addition of the New Generation Science Standards (NGSS). Again I find myself, our administration, and most of our teachers genuinely eager to incorporate them and hopefully further help student performances improve. According to its proponents, the Common Core State

Standards were adopted by forty-five states and the District of Columbia with the goal of "better preparing the nation's students for college or a job" by establishing "benchmarks for reading and math, replacing educational goals that varied widely from state to state" ("Guide to the Common Core" by Carolyn Thompson, 8-26-13, Associated Press). And even though the Common Core has been adopted and then un-adopted by select states' educational establishments and although conservative politicians have labeled the federally backed Common Core a violation of the Tenth Amendment's reserve clause, an infringement on the ideals of a state's right to run its own education system, "the standards spell out, grade by grade the reading and math skills that students should have as they go through high school" ("Guide to the Common Core").

State's rights' arguments aside and beyond the fact that it will be a boost across their education if we improve our students reading skills, if we take the Common Core goals seriously, they could open the gates to a far more inclusive and beneficial education system for all of our kids. More importantly, embracing the CCSS could address two very real problems we face in schools today. First, students with their ever-present electronics have instant access to all forms of data, making the traditional teaching methods of memorizing, repetition, and scaffolding to prepare for annual standard testing outdated. At one point in the history of our society, there was practical value in knowing and being able to recall data. Now the kids wonder, "Why should I bother to remember who the second President of the United States was when I can just Google it?" And they are right.

Second, though all the state taxpayers pay for it and all school- age children are legally required to attend, the school system today is designed to primarily serve the ultimate training needs of only a small percentage of our students, those who will attend and graduate from a four-year college. According to the Common Core State Standards Initiative (CCSS.com), the official home of the Common Core Standards hosted by the Council of Chief State Schools Officers and the National Center for Best Practices, "The Common Core is a set of high-quality academic standards in mathematics and English Language Arts (ELA) literacy. These learning goals outline what a student should know and be able to do at the end of each grade. The standards were created with the goal of "ensuring that all students graduate from high school with the skills and knowledge necessary to succeed in college, career, and life, regardless of where they live."

The biggest change the CCSS can bring to the educational system comes from the words "career and life." A handful of schools may have some programs to address these latter two goals, but, in general, schools see Non-college preparation programs (vocational training) as regressive to the students and demeaning to the schools themselves. In my school this year, out of 2,400 students, only 165 are enrolled in any type of "career training" (7 percent). No one wants to spend money nor exert energy on what is usually derisively called vocational education/ job training. But that is exactly what the majority of our students (72 percent) want and need.

The CCSS can also be a giant positive step in making our curriculum more up-to-date because its emphasis is no longer just on the retention of data that can be remembered to pass a standardized test once a year. On the contrary, under the stated goals of the Common Core, students are required to learn not only how to gather data but also how to analyze it and form conclusions about it alone and in group situations.

However, the cited goal that students be prepared "to succeed in college, career, and life, regardless of where they live" is far too large a goal if the way we try to reach it is limited to mathematics and English language arts goals as the standard state.

Here is the part of the Common Core standards that could do the most good for the most students. To be successful, to prepare our students to succeed in both college and career and, thus, make their legally mandated school years worthwhile for all our students, the Common Core program has to be massively larger and include all subjects.

It is still vitally important that as many students as wish to graduate from colleges and universities. We do need every student to be given a chance to become a physician, a lawyer, an engineer, or any other highly trained professional they want to be. However, that is not the complete story. The key statistics here are that according to the US Census report issued in 2012 for the 2010 Census, only 28 percent of Americans over twenty-five now hold or will likely ever hold at least a four-year college degree, and that figure was only slightly up from the 1995 Census report (from the 1990 Census) figure, which was 24.7 percent. It seems that whether the education hierarchy approves of it or not, the vast majority of Americans over many years have decided against going to and graduating from college, and we are still the most productive and competitive country in world markets. What those numbers tell us in the context of evaluating the success of our public education system is that instead of successfully preparing all of our children to lead full and productive lives according to their own desires, our schools are only even attempting to serve the needs of a small minority (28 percent) of our students, the college successful students. Conversely, these data also mean that we are leaving the majority of our children who are not interested in graduating from college, 72 percent of our students, unserved or underserved. Essentially, those seemingly surly, unproductive, and disconnected students we see in our classrooms every day, those kids who feel that their time in school is not worth the bother because, after four years of struggle and compliance, they will not be prepared to do any kind of work in the real world are exactly correct. When they leave high school, they will not be trained to do anything they or their parents see as useful to them. The travesty is that we are forcing students to toil for four years in high school with few to no marketable skills or abilities as a reward and then warehousing them for more years in what are called junior colleges, where so many of them will continue this fruitless process until when they are old enough and then decide to quit.

The Common Core demands that we do more. If we intend to "ensure that all students graduate from high school with the skills and knowledge necessary to succeed in college, career, and life," we need to both maintain the college-bound track benefits of a liberal arts education that teaches students to think imaginatively, that prepares them for college, while greatly enhancing the preparation of the 72 percent of our students whose choices require what school counselors today derisively call vocational training.

To accomplish this piece of the academic puzzle will require a dramatic change in education's institutional mindset and a demand by parents and other members of society. According to its own website, the Next Generation Science Standards were initiated in 2010 by the National Academy of Science, the National Association for the Advancement of Science, the National Science Teachers Association, and other related organizations when in 2010 they came to understand that "too few students were choosing to enter the leaky K-12 science, technology, engineering, and mathematics (STEM) talent pipe-line." They also came to support their choice to revamp Science

Standards because "never before has our world been so complex and scientific knowledge so critical to make sense of it all." In response, the scientific establishment decided that "we need new science standards that stimulate and build interest in STEM because science is central to the lives of all Americans" and because "all students, whether they become technicians in a hospital, workers in a high-tech manufacturing facility, or a PhD researcher, must have a solid K-12 science education." But what about the masses of our students who do not want to do any of those careers? The NGSS says that it, too, is focused on preparing students for college and careers and that it is aligned with what it calls the English/ Language Arts and Mathematics Common Core Standards, thereby serving both its own interests and those of students by "allowing for science to be part of a child's comprehensive education."

The current curriculum development process includes inputs chiefly from state boards of educators, teachers' groups, and elected school boards (the vast majority of whom have at least four-year degrees and, as such, carry a bias favoring college prep for all kids). For decades, these groups have been approving the books and curriculum and are seen to have done fairly well for the minority

28 percent of our students who do eventually graduate from four- year colleges, though this achievement, too, can be debatable, since according to the California State Regents, roughly 40 percent of incoming freshmen at CSU require some level of remedial education before continuing their work toward graduation. According to the National Conference of State Legislatures, "When considering all first-time undergraduates, studies have found between 28% to 40% of students take at least one remedial class." And "when looking at only community college students, (where a large majority of students go to continue) studies have found remediation rates surpassing 50%." According to Strong American Schools, the cost of this remediation can cost states and students up to $2.3 billion every year.

When it comes to the future of our children, whether we fully implement the Common Core or not, there are hard and practical choices to be made about each child, choices that should be made by a team of stakeholders surrounding the child and looking out for the best interests of both the child and of society as a whole. This group of stakeholders is what I call the child's educational convoy, borrowing the term from the protective process of American battleships defending supply and troop ships traveling across the North Atlantic during WWII from predatory submarines. Beginning in elementary school, each child's convoy/stakeholder team should consist of the child themselves as a full member (1), at least one of the child's parents (2), a representative of the elementary school they currently attend (3), and a representative of the middle school they are destined to attend (4), for a total of four. In middle school, the representative of the elementary school falls off, and we add the representative of the high school in their future (still four). In high school, the middle school representative falls off, and a representative of their future college or their job field is added.

Among the responsibilities of the members of the "convoy" will be to identify the things that the student enjoys doing, what they are good at. They should constantly be looking for subjects that will broaden the child's experience and increase their positive experiences in education. Beyond being productive, for each child, school should be enjoyable, even fun.

Continuing the theme of rewarding accomplishment, the six members of the stakeholder team (four current and two who dropped off during the journey) should be identified with the child (perhaps using their Social

Security numbers), and when the student achieves sought-after success for both themselves and society (as measured by their attaining and holding a job at the same company for two years after the end of their formal education), they should receive a one-time $200 to $500 tax deduction for their efforts.

The most difficult part of expanding the Common Core to reach its goal of preparing all students for "career and life" will be to identify what those needs are and then to understand how to address those needs and implement programs for the students. Being a stakeholder is not an easy job. If a student does not want to go to college, it has to be more than the afterthought it is now as to what background they will need. The stakeholders will have to come to a consensus within the local community as to what minimum a student should know and be able to do when he or she applies to a school or for a job. And this may be very difficult because each of the stakeholders may jealously hold very clear attitudes about what is and what certainly is "not their responsibility." We have to get beyond this. In fact, limited input from other stakeholders may be why public education is in the position we are in today, where only 28 percent of our students' needs are being addressed because no other group besides the colleges were invited to the discussion and allowed to participate. More realistically, if the student does not want to go on to college, we need to design a curriculum to meet the requirements of the businesses who will hire them, perhaps including mentorship programs, internships, and apprenticeships. For the nearly 72 percent of students who will not graduate from college nor want to get a college degree, industry leaders will have to become a large, if not dominant, part of the discussion. I would also include classes on proper behavior, proper dress, time management, and respect for others that will be helpful when today's students make the transition from the world of high school and children to the world of work and adult responsibility. If students see the work that they do in our classes as having a directly identifiable link to the real world of jobs and if the proof that they have those skills needs to be the student's successful passing of classes as appraised by the teacher (who may, in some cases, best be a representative of that hiring community), the atmosphere in today's schools will be far more productive and rewarding.

We, academics, who have never held those jobs, may believe that to be an auto mechanic or a plumber or a carpenter or a farmer, workers need only have training to do that job. But that would be wrong. Most of those jobs are becoming more and more complicated and technical, and the need for a mentally flexible workforce is increasing.

Yes, before the first student can begin the educational process, the student, the business community, the schools, and the parents have to agree and buy into what society needs for graduates to be able to do or what skills they need to have. And what else specifically should the student know or be able to do in order to better themselves or society before they get a diploma? The stakeholders will be empowered to identify what those needs are and at what age the student should come to master them before the student is sent along their agreed-to path of education.

Let's at least agree that the training and assimilation plan for every child should begin with reading, writing in English, as well as some competence at arithmetic. Assimilating every student should also mean teaching them a common history and making them familiar with such enlightening subjects as music or perhaps poetry and art. A working knowledge of economics and how their government works will also be helpful both to the graduate and to society.

Essentially, we should move away from the current "one

size fits all" series of graduation requirements, allowing for diversity based on the subject or path the individual student chooses. If the student wants to be a liberal arts teacher, his final requirement would be to prove he is able to explain concepts to others and perform more liberal arts projects and perhaps less math. If the student wants to be some form of scientist, there should be more math and direct lab sciences, less testing on symbolism in literature. However, if the student wants to avoid higher academic education in favor of a trade, he should be held to the standards for that choice, which may or may not include upper math skills or a philosophical knowledge of Moby Dick and Hester Prynne. How much science the students are required to take should also be made on an individual basis. The stakeholders will have to choose what the proper mix is for their students.

There should always be meaningful and immediate rewards for each grade level achieved within the system. This could be as simple as having designated juniors- or seniors-only lawn areas for lunch. No little kids allowed. It could also mean bandannas, badges, and caps designating the best achievers as the students advance. Heroes should be heralded. Graduating students also need to be well- rounded citizens ready to take on the rights and rewards and also the responsibilities that come with their accomplishments.

So-called social promotions should be made illegal. If there is an issue with the child completing the necessary skill acquisition, the problem should be remedied before the child moves to the next level. We owe these children the experience of overcoming difficult circumstances that we rob them of if we simply "blink and let them pass."

It does take a village to raise and educate a child, and all the stakeholders will need to help determine what it means to have the knowledge "necessary to succeed in college, career, and life" that the Common Core Standards espouses for all public school systems. And it could be an expensive process to upgrade facilities, but if the additional training needed for the non-college students is not supplied and then included in graduation requirements, the Common Core's goal and perhaps the whole concept of public education itself is a farce from the beginning. And if a life-practical level of vocational training is to become a valued part of the educational mix, there needs to be a dramatic attitudinal change in the current school mindset to one where this training is equally valued.

What else specifically should the student know or be

able to do in order to better themselves or society before they get a diploma? All of today's students, even those who do not want to go to college, are the adult citizens of tomorrow and deserve training beyond the limits of their vocational field. If the highest level of free public schooling is to be the twelfth grade, a senior in high school, in addition to possessing the skills required to be hired into an entry- level position in some industry, must be prepared to join society as a young, educated American.

The heart of the system should be that all along the way, advancing students (even with a team of advocates behind them) must be made to prove in some way that they have the communally required skills before they are awarded the next advancement and eventually a diploma. Helping students achieve these goals should be the prime function of teachers. However, the "evidence" that the students could use to prove themselves should only rarely be in the form of a formal written test. If the world of education is to be made more practical, "practical" exams should be the order of the day, such as if a student wants to be an auto mechanic, he could be given a car with known problems and then have him diagnose and fix the problems, or a would-be hairdresser can show their skill on a cooperative head, or perhaps the evidence for another line of work could be the passing of their classes and a portfolio evidencing the work they have done or the passing of their classes and an interview between the graduation candidate and non-parental representatives of the community. The ways the students can prove their skills are again up to the stakeholders.

In short, the stakeholders will have to take on the responsibility of choosing what the proper mix is for their children/students. Training our children for their future is too important a mission for the schools alone to carry.

In a scenario where students and their parents are among the stakeholders because they have been in on the planning all along, every child will know exactly why they are in each class and exactly what skills or abilities they are expected to acquire in that class. It would also help set priorities for the teachers. Imagine a world where all students leaving high school are prepared for and have connections with people who will hire them for good-paying jobs after graduation, where fast food companies will have to raise the wages they pay, not as a matter of generosity or in response to public pressure because the cost of living for their employees is getting too high and the local city is pressed to pass laws raising the minimum wage but because those employees and future employees will have the required skills to get and hold better, higher-paying jobs.

And just what will we do with the children who do not achieve the prescribed target skills on the schedule set out for them? All of their stakeholders and society itself need to muster all our capabilities to help the child achieve what they need to. However, as of today, the ultimate responsibility has to belong to the student, and the stakeholders must also act in the interest of society and not allow the reward of graduation to go to students who do not earn it. In the schools today, we often socially advance students so that they can stay up with their same-age peers and hope they have a chance to achieve the goals over time. The problem being, if they never run into a wall of non-progression, if the students are never "failed," an ever-increasing number will again arrive at the end of high schools with the same lack of skills and, therefore, a level of unpreparedness at least as high as we have today. But if there is a problem, be it a language barrier or a mental incapability, under a multiple stakeholder process, the issue should be identified and addressed at its earliest appearance. Passing a problem on to the next year and the next teacher should never be allowed.

However, as we have seen with other attempts to change our bureaucratic system, block scheduling or Schools within Schools, seemingly simple-to-fix problems can be used to defeat the change. Hopefully, fifty states and thousands of stakeholders afraid of change will not kill the good that can come out of the Common Core with the pain of a thousand small cuts. The Common Core can be the tool we use to identify the changes to the current system that need to be made. It can be used to identify and strengthen both the path of college-bound students and those who choose another path. However, it has to be a major change, perhaps even bigger than the most enthusiastic proponent has in mind. The stakeholders (those who will both achieve and benefit from the change) will need to identify what those needs are and at what age the student should come to master them before the student is sent along their agreed to path. Then the WASC process can be used to ensure that the Common Core goals are being implemented.

CHAPTER 17

Q: What Is WASC?

A: WASC, as the enforcement arm of the Common Core WASC partnership, could be the single most important direct incentive to keep schools in America constantly improving.

ACCORDING TO ITS WEBSITE, WASC (Western Association of Schools and Colleges), with its assessment arm, the Accrediting Commission for Schools (ACS), is a world-renown accrediting association that works alongside education-minded organizations across the country and worldwide to "help schools identify and implement school improvement needs and support accountability" (www. wasc.org). WASC ACS extends its services to over 4,600 schools, whether the schools are public, independent, church- related, adult schools, or proprietary Pre-K-12, and consists of thirty-two representatives from the educational organizations that it serves. These include the Association of California School Administrators, the California Department of Education, the California School Boards Association, the California Charter Schools Association, as well as the California Federation of Teachers, and the California Teachers Association.

The school evaluations are based on three philosophical pillars: first, that a school's goal must be that of successful student learning; second, that each school must have a clear purpose and schoolwide student goals; and third, schools must engage in external and external evaluations as part of continued school improvement in support of student learning.

To be seen as worthwhile by students and the local community, the public schools must challenge the students to improve their skill levels in ways that will be helpful to their future inside as well as outside the world of academics and to do this in an environment of constant change. This is where programs like WASC can serve a vital need. Getting a high rating on its WASC evaluation, proving to outside visitors who are traveling education experts from an array of other districts that you have evaluated and updated your institutional goals and that you can show evidence that you are working on the issues and are improving your programs to the benefit of your student's learning can be a monstrously difficult thing for a school to accomplish, and not every school earns a high WASC ranking. However, by scoring well, a school can prove to itself, its students, and the community (i.e., all the stakeholders) that it is the option-exploring and mind-developing place all today's stakeholders need and want them to be (a place where the effort students put in leads to a real and evident benefit to them and to their community).

Like most bureaucracies, schools naturally focus on what they do fairly well—in the case of the school system, to use academics to prepare students for more academics (i.e., high schools that lead to colleges)—and then they concentrate on improving themselves in their own selected area of expertise. (They know what they do well, and they want to do it better.) However, as noted before, schools today have an institutional bias against what they derisively refer to as vocational training, and they don't serve all their stakeholders well. And that bias, like institutional racism or sexism, is widespread and deep. Students who do not elect to go the "college track" route are thought to be very sad stories, even losers. At my school, the counseling department prides itself as being solely "academic counselors," perhaps not understanding the limitations to our students of that title and attitude. Identifying this problem can be a major benefit of the Common Core. To force the schools to face it and eliminate the problem is the work of WASC.

However, changing out of an established mindset is never easy, and the schools will not likely make the philosophic and expensive changes necessary without prodding. However, if the Common Core process can identify what needs to be done school by school and WASC can be used to force the changes to be made, they could be the tools that make our free public education serve all those involved. All the different segments of "We the People" could get the education that they want and that we need.

Describing their own added value to the schools and other stakeholders, WASC explains that "accreditation is integral to a school's perpetual cycle of assessment, planning, implementation, monitoring, and reassessment based upon student achievement." In addition, they state that the evaluation process encourages school improvement through a process of "continuing evaluation and recognizing, by accreditation, schools that meet an acceptable level of quality in accordance with established criteria." Furthermore, WASC says that its goals are to assure local communities that the schools have a "viable education program," that each is a "trustworthy institution for student learning," and that the accreditation process also "validates the integrity of the school's program and transcripts." Overall, WASC's goal is to "foster the ongoing improvement of the school's programs and operations to support student learning."

The main argument against the WASC ACS process is that it requires literally thousands of work hours be spent by each school over two to three years in order to catalogue the school's objectives and to collect the appropriate data that will prove the school is doing at least an adequate job of achieving those objectives and educating its students. The objection being that all this very expensive time spent analyzing the school's processes is time taken away from the school's main function, teaching its students. To be as thorough as the ACS demands and to instill the sense of teamwork, which will make continuing the process over a period of years possible, requires the time and effort of the administrators, the teachers, the clerical and other staff, and, of course, the parents and the students themselves. My school's 2016 WASC report is 418 pages long, consisting of five chapters and an appendix.

Chapter 1, "Community and Student Profiles," is a broad profile of the location of the school and the socioeconomic background of its community, as well as the school's vision statement, mission statement, and the identification of the major concern of the ACS from the previous 2010 WASC visit that even though the school was awarded a second consecutive six-year accreditation, all be it with an interim visit after a few years, my school needed to "better show evidence that the school was improving student achievement." The school's response was to use the academic performance index (API) to gather data to assess our progress toward increased literacy and academic success for all students. Chief among the available data sources would be the STAR testing process (now defunct), the also now discontinued California High School Exit Exam (CAHSEE), as well as student, parent, and staff surveys with appropriate findings.

Chapter 2, "Progress Since Last WASC," since

the previous WASC report (2010) had awarded our school a six-year accreditation (the best score allowed), but with another three-year interim visit, the 2016 recommendations were to basically keep doing what we are doing, and do more of it, yet adding to the mix the implementation of the Common Core Standards the development of common assessments and benchmarks within departments, and to assure that every department show evidence of implementing academic language strategies with all students. The chapter includes descriptions of how these recommendations are being actively addressed.

Chapter 3, "Analysis of Profile," is an opportunity for the school to "explain the implications of the collected data with respect to student performance." Since we have been involved in the WASC process for many years, we were focused on and are able to prove that we as a school have conducted annual reviews and analyses of student data and have developed an action plan to identify what we are doing right, as well as what areas we need to work on. Continuing to quote the 2016 report, the staff and stakeholders of my school "are very pleased with the student performance data as reflected by our API and CAHSEE scores, as well as increasing graduation rates, completion of the A-G requirements, decreasing drop-out rates and the reduction of suspensions and expulsions. Improvements in student performances are a direct result of the hard work and support of the staff and Administration." But as to the value add of the WASC process, the answer is quite simple. At my school, "WASC enables us to celebrate our successes and work on our areas of need."

Chapter 4, "Self-Study Report," began with prompts and indicators taken directly from the 2015 version of the manual produced by WASC to help schools analyze and report on their own situations. My school responded by having our staff break into five voluntary focus groups, each given the opportunity as a group and individually to add their perspective on what has been happening at our school site as well as to what they considered our strengths and the areas where we can improve. This section is 225 pages long.

Chapter 5, "Action Plan," identifies the three goals we have chosen to address in the immediate future— first that our students will achieve at high levels based on standards set by the Common Core State Standards, Next Generation Science Standards, and School- wide Learner Outcomes; second, to improve the assessment scores of our historically identified underperforming student populations as well as students struggling outside these subgroups; and third, to improve college and career guidance services to all our students. For each of these goals, this chapter describes the rationale behind the goal, what indicators will be used to measure our results, the tasks involved, the responsible party(s), and a timeline.

The "Appendix" consists of a glossary and thirty-six pages of charts and graphs, the results from surveys given to students (Appendix B, 39 items), parents (Appendix C, 42 items), and the school staff (Appendix D, 63 items), which together indicate the participants' opinions concerning the school's people, academics, and environment.

Predictably the results gleaned from the surveys are neither all positive nor all negative but are an honest indication of how each set of stakeholders really feel about their school, adding to our knowledge of how we can improve.

The WASC ACS process could perhaps be the single most important direct incentive to keep schools in America great because a successful accreditation takes a lot of work on the part of the school, and it is difficult to achieve. The process forces organizations to take a hard look at what they are doing and then forces them to prove what they have accomplished to outside visitors. Not all schools do well under the scrutiny a WASC visit entails, and everyone should be aware of the failures as well.

If handled properly, what can make the task worth the bother is that when we create a challenging atmosphere where the school is known to be highly successful and where success achieved begets an expectation of future success, all the stakeholders tend to feel empowered and to be due the respect earned by that collective achievement.

What we and other schools do not do at all well with WASC is making our achievements public. In the case of my school, we earned and were awarded a full six-year accreditation for three consecutive attempts, yet very few people are aware of the success. If we were a sports team and we achieved our goal of earning a six-year accreditation (or a championship) for three consecutive seasons, there would be major television coverage, speeches, and a call from the President (in our case, maybe an in-person address to the staff by the district superintendent, a banner headline in the local newspaper, and perhaps even a mention on the school website—none of which ever happened). Every player, every student, and every spectator, when they entered our arena, should be made aware of and feel the pride for what we have earned, and they might even feel the need to work hard to become part of our community. The sense of pride and mutual respect should become the norm. However, schools and people who work at schools do not seem to feel worthy of acclaim, especially if it requires that they "toot their own horns." However, this reluctance to shout our own praises results in the value of the school experience going unknown. The problem is that today communities and students themselves are becoming more troublesome, in part because they do not appreciate nor respect the value added to their lives by the schools and those who work there. Accomplishment should be brazenly announced and widely known for education as it is in professional sports.

CHAPTER 18:

Conclusions

Q: What Can We Do Today?

A: Let's get radical.

IF THERE IS ANYTHING that the American experience shows us, it's that change is inevitable and that railing against change is futile. The changes we need to fix our education system will require determination and institutional courage, but it is no less than the future of our children in the balance. School hierarchies and school districts are like large ships, and they do not easily change directions. Even faced with a growing number of unmotivated, nonproductive, and rebellious school children and an increasing shortage of teachers, I suspect that the education bureaucracy will be hesitant and slow to make the major changes necessary for a complete Common Core implementation. Why is that? For one thing, it's about money. Hiring and training people and building facilities will be expensive. But an even larger and more pervasive problem is the fear that any corrective action, any requirement that students actually learn enough to add value to society, will raise the dropout rate, and with it, the ire of parents and communities, and probably evoke a wave of lawsuits.

The schools will assume that the teachers will do as they always have (i.e., make the best of an increasingly difficult situation), and the districts will do as much as they think they can do without upsetting anyone. Schools are staffed by very nice people who want to be seen as doing as much as possible to ensure that every child succeeds. In short, if there is a problem today or if any given child is not succeeding, the school believes that it is primarily the school's responsibility to address the problem and to find a solution that is acceptable to the child, their parents, and the outside community. The education system's working philosophy is that free public education is the natural right of all children and should require only the most minimal of efforts on the part of the student. Standards, accordingly, are set so low that no student can be allowed to fail.

This ideal translates to a situation today where, if a child in school decides not to do the things he or she is asked to do in a class and as a result, they fail that class, the education system does not hold the child responsible but swings into action to find something easier for them to do instead, and then easier still until the students are not required to learn any more than a very low minimum in the process and yet they can be moved along the educational path. And let's be clear, the public school system today is not designed to prepare the children for a brighter future. The educational system is designed to provide nothing more than "a pipeline" where most students enter it and are processed through without a hitch. But even then, students who do not perform to even a minimum standard, who do not succeed even in this lax environment, and who do not move on to the next level increase the total cost of education and plug up the pipeline. As for teachers, even though they are the ones supposedly held responsible to maintain the rigor and the requirements of each of their classes, the schools and the school districts demand a zero dropout rate. And the very last thing a school system established to move masses of students through in a smooth process wants is for some "difficult" teacher to have standards that are higher than absolutely necessary before their students advance. In schools, this costly obstruction shows up as students repeating classes that the school has already been paid for them to have passed.

To be worth the money spent, each class has to be rigorous enough to eventually improve the student's ability to add value to society, which should be the goal of a public education symbolized by a high school diploma. But experience tells us that the nonproductive student will only pass the class if one of two scenarios occurs. First, it will happen if doing so is or can become important to the student, their parents, and the community. It can also happen if the teacher makes the class so easy that passing it requires little or nothing of the student and adds the same little or nothing to the betterment of society. To one extent or another, that conflict is seen in every classroom in America today.

Every year, however, during graduation ceremonies, when the teachers are all sitting as a group aside the stage, one of our vice principals will stipulate to a ranking district officer that each of the graduates present that day has achieved the necessary "requirements for graduation." In some cases, every year with some "graduates," his or her teachers look at each other and wonder, since our classes are graduation requirements and we know the child did not pass our class as recently as that day, how can they be walking the stage?

In many cases, the answer is that the student has been allowed to bypass the requirements. If a student today chooses not to do assigned work or learn the required skill and fails a required class, one solution is that he can take the twenty-week semester class over again in a three-to six-week summer session for the same number of units toward graduation. And if he fails or chooses not to participate in the summer session or if he needs the units to graduate sooner than the end of the summer session, he can take an online class called Cyber High, which reportedly requires even less. The good news for the school is that the student throughput remains high, and the dropout rates remain low. It's little wonder that today too many high school students meet graduation requirements, yet, according to the office of the Chancellor of the University of California (as reported earlier), 40 to 50 percent of our "graduates" require remedial classes before they are prepared to take college classes.

The sad reality today is, if the parent or the child with so few units earned comes into the counselor's office or if the counselor with up to a 1,200 child workload notices this child is unlikely to graduate, there are even more "lower the dropout rate" programs to help them make up enough credits. Yes, they can attend summer school, take the online classes of Cyber High, or even take classes at a local community college. In the past, they have even been allowed to spend time after school filling out subject matter packets at a rate of so many graduation units per packet, no exams or learning required. In the past few years, faced with a growing number of unmotivated, nonproductive, and rebellious school-children, we have actually established and staffed whole "credit recovery schools" whose sole purpose is to help children make up credits that for whatever reason they did not earn in their regular classes. The children have to be down a substantial number of credits in order to qualify to go there, but these schools exist, and there are waiting lists of students trying to get in. Then when, through whatever magic of lowered expectations, these students "earn" enough credits to get close to graduation requirements, they are transferred back to their original school to be graduated with their original class. And it's getting worse over time. The educational system's willingness to go over and above to "help" as many students meet graduation requirements as possible, thus keeping the dropout rate as low as possible, reduces the likelihood that the individual child, when intellectually challenged, will do what is required of them in their regular classes. "Why should I? I can just take it in Cyber High, and it's easier there." Good question.

A true story—during the spring semester of 2015, one of the young men in my Economics class, which is a semester class that is a graduation requirement for seniors, was not having difficulty in the class but simply stopped attending. It's not his name, but I'll call him Ben. Week after week went by, and other students would report that they had seen Ben on campus, yet he didn't come to class. He obviously missed all the tests and assignments, and he didn't show up for the final exam (which for seniors was given a week earlier than for the other classes; this semester, it was on a Thursday.) The day after the finals (Friday, as I was cleaning up my classroom for the summer), Ben walked into my room with a tale of woe and told me that he had relatives coming to town from a long way away just to see him graduate. Was there anything he could do to make up the work? I liked Ben a lot, and it was difficult for me, but I had to be fair to the ninety other students who had come to class, done the assignments, and passed the class. I told Ben, "No. It's too late." He seemed to have accepted responsibility for his own situation, yet crestfallen, Ben thought of a way out—Cyber High. By sitting down at the computer for a few hours, he could make up the graduation units that passing my class would have given him. It has been the policy of my school since the invention of Cyber High that students were not allowed to take Cyber High to make up for a class they were currently enrolled in and were failing. If not for this policy, every child having difficulty in any class would take the far easier path and never learn what he should have in the regular classroom. However, on the following Monday, Ben came back to my room to share with me that his counselor had denied his request but that he escalated it to the principal, who approved it. Estimating that it would take a few hours of computer work over two days, what he later called "so easy it was waste of my time," on graduation day, Ben was there, wearing his cap and gown and brandishing his new diploma. His out-of-town relatives would see Ben graduate but may never realize what part of his education he had been deprived of.

Why should students do anything that challenges them? It's so much easier for them if they don't. This process of giving students rewards, even when they do not earn them, is the main reason we have an "achievement gap" in America. Awarding high school diplomas for work not done is a formula for disaster, not the way to create achievement-oriented young people who learn that they can and must survive by contributing to society. If we love these kids, we should prepare them for what is ahead of them. It is hard out there in the world, and it's not all about them. The real world expects our future adults to earn a living and to do that by contributing to society.

We in schools should stop covering for failure and promote success. Graduation diplomas should be denied to those who do not earn them. We are robbing our kids of confidence and the feeling of satisfaction that only comes when they accomplish something that is not easy, that is not given to them. If they do not do their job, their employer will fire them. Inevitably, they will be held accountable for what they do and don't accomplish. Are we doing them any favors by letting them expect that the world out there is determined to make their lives as easy and effort-free as their school was?

What we are doing in schools today is analogous to

rearranging the deck chairs on the *Titanic*. What we need is a barrier against icebergs. Using the jargon of pre-WWII supply of England against the Nazis, we need an "educational convoy" system.

Let's get really radical. *Now!*

We should immediately change the emphasis within the educational system to one where each student's accomplishments are celebrated in smaller steps and where there are expanded rewards for achieving the next higher class ranking. In high school, there should be a major celebration on their advancing to their sophomore, junior, and senior years, official banquets served by lowerclassmen, or a trip to a nearby amusement park for the day. The school should pay for it, but only if the students earn the units required to attain the reward under normal classroom conditions. Let's either do away with summer school, Cyber High, and other programs designed to make up for failing classes, or at the very least make them worth fewer credits so that taking them does not equate to the same benefit as students would garner from passing actual classes. These "makeup units" structures are simply lies that tell our kids that it's okay not to try and that failure has no consequences. In a worst case scenario, being a "fourth-year freshman" (having attended school for four years but not earning enough credits to be designated even a sophomore) should be an uncomfortable circumstance which both students and their families should struggle to avoid. The summit of the free public education process, graduation from high school, should be a major event celebrating accomplishment, not mediocrity or the mere passage of four years.

There should be lavish incentives for those who succeed, perhaps even money payments for great grades, either in cash or credits toward college. What if, for those students who want to go to college, by the time they graduate from high school, they could have earned enough financial incentive and support in the form of a voucher to pay for college or at least make it cheaper? Perhaps for students entering the workforce, enough money to pay a month or two's rent while they move out of Mama's house after they begin their new job. That would have both an immediate short-term and long-term positive effect on both the student and their family and also on society and the colleges themselves who would be getting students who were prepared to succeed. And for those critics who would argue against putting the stain of humiliation on a non- achiever, I would say that the schools will help them in every way possible but that in the end, if the student and their parents choose not to make use of the opportunity to get a free education, their choice should be respected. I would also ask, won't those children and their families go through more suffering if they are continuously allowed to leave high school unprepared to face the world? An effective incentive to achieve now could improve their lives.

We need college-educated people, engineers, and scientists to make life better and to compete with other countries; certainly, we do. But not every child with half an aptitude for school has to go to college. We already know that the vast majority of students have no interest in completing a four-year degree and never have had. As noted in earlier chapters, the fact is that only about 28 percent of Americans today (according to the US Census Report issued 2012) have four-year degrees or higher, and that number hasn't changed significantly in fifty years. What that means is that 72 percent of Americans have lived perfectly fine, productive lives without a college degree, and we did win the Cold War, and we are still the world's number one country as far as inventive technology.

On the other hand, I live in the San Francisco Bay

Area, and it's expensive to live here. If our children are going to survive in this world economically, they need training. Basically, they need to learn to do something that someone will be willing to pay them a lot of money to do. We need the college-educated, but we also need mechanics and plumbers and carpenters and farmers. We need the Roto-Rooter man and cooks in our restaurants.

We should stop telling our students that people who don't go to college are losers, which is exactly what we do tell them. High school counselors today fancy themselves as "academic counselors" and push any student with a minimal talent for school into at least a junior college. And that's wrong. What we have today in California and other states is a community college system that is severely overcrowded with students who are only there because they are not prepared to or interested in getting a job, and their parents will still support them if they are "in college." Then after three or four years living with their parents, paying ever-increasing fees (which the higher education system is only too eager to accept and which Presidential candidates for 2020 are running on a proposal for the taxpayer to pay their tuition in total), attending classes, and still not attaining any useful skills, they quit going, and if they're lucky, they find a job they were qualified to have immediately after high school. "Would you like fries with that?"

We owe our kids better than what they are getting. Students should have legitimate choices to go to college or not to, but for their own reasons. For the billions of dollars we are paying, having gone to high school, every student should be equipped with a clear idea of what the next step is for them to being a full economic citizen, where they can hope to achieve the American dream of a home with a white picket fence, a spouse or life partner, and perhaps children.

Today newspapers are filled with stories about fast-food workers striking for a minimum wage they can live on. The minimum wage only contributes positively to people who, though hardworking, do not have the necessary skills to get a higher-paying job. The debate should not be an argument between how much a person needs to make in order to survive, nor if Americans who need help to survive should get that help. Rather, if students were trained in high school with skills they could live on, Micky D's and most other minimum wage employers would have to raise their pay scales to compete and attract anyone to work there. The answer is not to raise the minimum wage; that's a temporary patch over a system failure. We need to provide a more capable workforce that has earned and is qualified for more and better opportunities.

It would cost nothing and could be done immediately if we simply accepted the fact that not all children have to or should go to college. But then, it will likely require a major investment to develop training systems to prepare those who do not. At any rate, what we should have learned by now is that forcing further education on students who do not want it is like teaching a pig to dance—it's really hard to do, and it annoys the pig.

It's a fine thing to help students succeed; however, states and school districts need to reestablish rigorous educational goals that not only challenge the student but also serve to help improve society. They also must have the courage to put teeth in these goals and only reward those students who truly earn them. And if what the students learn were to truly prepare them for a future of their choice, we will all be better off, and the respect that society gives to the teachers who help them accomplish what is truly in their own and societies' best interest will be commensurately higher.

America truly does feel a malaise about our schools, but the question is, does America have both the courage and the determination to rethink what we are doing in education and to make dramatic changes to accomplish the goal of having all our successful students graduate from high school with the skills and knowledge necessary to succeed in college, career, and life?

If the majority of people in American society can understand that the teaming up of the Common Core and WASC may be the best opportunity we are likely to get in order to really change things for all our children's betterment, this period of malaise can be converted into a time of exploration of the possible, with dynamic and positive changes.

What does it come down to? What are we doing to prepare our children for their chosen futures? In my subjects—History, Economics, and Government—the goal of the class has always come down to the use of redundant systems (called scaffolding) in order to increase the odds of the student recalling data for a standardized test and then perhaps for their lives. In this evaluation process, the more the students remember that day, the better the school and the teacher are deemed to have performed. This reflects the fact that, in the past, if people needed to know things in their personal or "real" life, it was helpful to remember the data. (The capital of California is Sacramento. How many electrons does a hydrogen atom have? And a noun is a person, place, animal, or thing.) In times past, if we remembered the data, we would not have to spend the time or expend the effort to go to a library or to a book to look it up. A good memory was a "value add" to us personally and to society.

In contrast, our children today have instant information at their fingertips (or at least at their thumb tips). In their future, there will be no "value added" to have a great memory. If they need to know data, they will Google it. So if not to teach children to learn or remember things, in the future, what will be the function of schools? The answer is twofold: continued assimilation and training for their future.

And what should the process look like to achieve those aims?

First, let's provide every child with an educational convoy, a team of interested stake-holders surrounding every child entering elementary school. These stakeholders should include the child themselves as a full member, their parents, a representative of the elementary school they are joining, and a representative of the middle school, which is their next step in the process. The main function of each child's team of stakeholders is to spend the year getting to know the child and to encourage and support their learning to deal with as vast an array of positive experiences as they can and to find out what the child likes and what they are good at. These experiences could be anything—from the joy of numbers, the wizarding world of science, to how stuff works together for the future engineer or mechanic. And the meeting of the team should happen at least once a year or as things change.

All of these people have a stake in the success of that child's scholastic future and should be in on the development of a plan for them to succeed and to be prepared for their next step in society. The main question is, what should the child need to be able to do to function well, not at the end of their career but at the next level? This knowledge should include both scholastic (reading, writing, and math levels) and social skills and citizenship. There are skills required to get along with others and to work in a group. Honesty and integrity should also be expected and, therefore, taught.

Depending on how the district or the school decide to staff for this increased responsibility, there could be between a few and very many new positions opening at each school site, whose new hires would be available to advocate for new or enhanced programs, experiences, and trainings for their individual charges. The whole school experience could become very dynamic and be honed to serve the individual needs of each child in very practical ways, which in time could alter the outflow of caring and qualified teachers, becoming an inflow of professionals interested in doing exactly what is in the best interests of everyone.

During the student's last year of elementary school, another meeting should take place, this time, between new stakeholders (the student, their parent, the middle school they will attend next, and this time a representative of the high school that middle school will feed into). In middle school, the emphasis should be on both exploring new areas of study and developing further the child's already identified interests. The point of the exercise is to map out a program for this child that helps with any shortcoming he has encountered and a program that ensures the student is prepared to enter and succeed in high school.

Finally, each student will have the last of their stakeholders' meetings with themselves, their parents, a representative of the high school, and this time a representative of the college or university or a representative of the industry the student plans to work in. In high school, the mission of the team of stakeholders will be to assist the student in choosing their next path to the future and then gaining the training needed to achieve their goals. At any rate, if the team succeeds, each student would leave the public school system with every possible opportunity to have "the skills and knowledge necessary to succeed in college, career, and life."

CHAPTER 19

Q: Covid-19, its history, and its effect on society and the schools?

A: Covid-19 has been both massive and deadly on society and especially on our schools.

"DOUBLE, DOUBLE TOIL AND trouble/fire burn and caldron bubble." – Macbeth

The Covid virus has been a widespread and deadly curse on the world and on America. Worldwide, 4,667,000 people have died of the infection. (worldometers.info) More than 666,000 Americans have died (Johns Hopkins University), which is more than the 625,000 Americans who died in our most deadly conflict, the American

Civil War. (Militaryfactory.com) However, the deadly contagion has simply been layered over the conflicts and growing hatreds already vexing American society.

Americans have seen and felt the pain of racial strife that has raged and simmered for hundreds of years. Some people consider that things on the racial front have improved; others, especially those who feel minimized or damaged, admit that there has been movement, but not enough, and not fast enough to establish equality. The historic fact is that our Constitution was written by fallible men who agreed to institutionalize human slavery in The United States of America in order to accomplish the creation of the new country. Today that internalized suffering acts out as rioting, looting, and the burning of buildings in response to the publicized abuse of power by a small number of policemen. And politicians are only too happy to take advantage of the situation.

Our two party political system strives to give voice to many conflicting factions, allowing each its "15 minutes of fame" as a means of "letting off steam" and avoiding a major explosion. But in combination, it appears that the country is coming apart at the seams while our political leaders are frozen in their own struggle to discredit and destroy their opposition. We read about a time in the past when opposing party members would argue and debate their differences by day and then sit down for a friendly brew in the evening. That possibility seems unlikely in today's political climate as the hostility between factions seems to be getting worse.

On the home front, so-called "social media" allows for unkind and unloving people to hide behind their own anonymity, in front of their computers, and spew out all manner of partial truths and blatant lies to their followers and whoever will listen to support their beliefs or add strife and hatred to the political discourse.

Though it's easy to conclude that today's strife within our country is as bad as it has ever been, we have been through these times before, and we have made corrections and adapted to the needs of those involved. For instance: In the days of the American Revolution, our "forefathers" and our "foremothers" also formed factions within their society. At the time of the Declaration of Independence, the colonists were deeply divided. It is estimated that a third wanted freedom from Great Britain, another third remained loyal to King George III, and the last third were busy with their lives. However, beliefs were strong and strident. And politics became personal and dirty. Public figures such as Alexander Hamilton and Andrew Jackson brought down the lightning by offering their ideas of how the new nation should be run. Human sentiments of right and wrong and honor became enflamed to the point that, as the new country fought to establish itself, Democratic Republican Vice President Burr shot and killed Federalist Alexander Hamilton in a duel that was as much about politics as about circulated personal letters.

Andrew Jackson was denied his first popular victory in the election of 1824, as his political opposition engaged in what became known as "The Corrupt Bargain," and Jackson himself would blame the death of his wife Rachel in 1828, the year he was elected President, on the pressures of dirty politics.

Thirty-two years later, in 1860, the political issues of the day were slavery and the right of those states who created the Union to dissolve it. Party power politics could not or did not find a solution, and as a result, 630,000 people died in the American Civil War. Eventually, the 13th, 14th, and 15th Amendments to the Constitution would legally eliminate the sin of slavery, make each former slave an American citizen, and give each black man the right to vote.

Today, we have factions; and our points of pride and beliefs about right and wrong seem to grow more fervent and more brittle by the week. Racial factions, Right and Left political factions, and economic divisions have divided the citizenry and frozen our political leaders. Our schools were becoming a reflection of the coarsening of society and were struggling to cope. Then came the epidemic.

Prior to 2019, we had not heard of nor understood that a deadly pandemic was enveloping the world and headed for our shores, a virus that would not only completely shut down our schools but also much of the American and world economy. The thing we cannot lose sight of is that, though Covid-19 has become the headline, issues such as racial and political turmoil, lack of respect, and subsequent low morale among teachers, and the lack of preparation for the students' futures still exist, making the school experience even more of a horror story for our students, teachers, and a questionable investment for taxpayers. So, how did the effects of Covid-19 come about so quickly? The information here is compiled chiefly from the CDC, the NEA, and Education Week.

The virus originally named "Corona Virus 2019 (Corona-19)" by the World Health Organization was first detected in China in December of 2019. Thought to have originated in a province called Wuhan, the deadly infection has grown to nearly a million cases across 200 countries. And it would not be easy to defeat; according to the National Institutes of Health, the virus remained "stable for several hours to days in aerosols or on surfaces," perfect to be spread through small environments like classrooms and offices.

As of January 29, 2020, there were only five reported cases of the virus in the US. Eventually, it would spread to 48 states, affecting million public school children. At first, the plan was to close schools "temporarily" for a thorough cleaning of surfaces and airways. On February 11, teacher's unions called for Federal guidance concerning handling the virus. By mid-February, Washington state and New York were temporarily closing schools for cleaning. On February 25, the CDC warned all schools to prepare for the virus. On February 27, Bethel High School in Washington state became the first school to shut down, in this case, for two days of disinfecting. On March 5, the North Shore school district in Washington state announced that it would close the schools in their district for fourteen days. However, it would not be that simple.

On March 5, 2020, the WHO declared what came to be called Covid-19 to be an epidemic. March 12, Ohio became the first state to announce state-wide school closures, and one day later, 15 more states closed their schools. By March 16, 27 states had halted all in- person instruction for the rest of the school year. Other states would follow quickly. By March 25, almost all US public schools were closed for the remainder of the school year. The only exceptions were Montana and Wyoming. On April 8, a survey of public school teachers reported that 66% said that morale was lower than it was, even before the virus. As of August 24, 2021, 1013 active and retired k-12 teachers had died.

On August 12, 2021, the NEA published a press release claiming that 90% of its members were vaccinated and declared their support for all educators to receive Covid-19 vaccinations or submit to regular testing. As the 2021-22 school year begins, the NEA encourages "wide spread use of safe and effective vaccinations for educators and students."

So, where do we go from here? How do we as a people accept, even encourage our differences, and work together for a common better world, where teachers and schools provide what their students need for a productive future, are respected for doing so, and where the necessary police power is both valued and supervised? But mainly, how do we create an evolving society where every American feels so deeply respected within themselves that we are not so easily offended by people we encounter?

Today in America, we have seen rioting and insurrections on a local scale, in places like Portland and Washington D.C., but we are not on the verge of Civil War, and the institutions we have created have dealt with or adapted to the underlying issues. Yet, according to a survey done by the American Psychological Association and published in the Washington Post: 69% of Americans are stressed about the future of America.

In the "land of the free and the home of the brave" where each individual has the right and the inherent obligation to live in and to rectify conditions in his community first, and then in combination with others, the country, we should all look within ourselves for that spark that God has placed there. Being a Christian, I look within and to the scriptures. When asked by the leaders of the time which of the Commandments is the greatest concerning how people should live, Jesus answered them, saying, "Thou shalt love the Lord, thy God, with all thy heart, and with all thy soul, and with all thy mind. This is the first and the greatest Commandment. And the second is like it. Thou shalt love thy neighbor as thyself." (Mathew 22: 36-40)

The first step is to understand that God is inherently good, He loves us, and that He is worthy of our love. The second step is to understand that as we walk through our lives, we are all quick to rationalize and forgive ourselves for doing questionable, even bad things. We need to be equally quick to understand and to forgive others in the same way. In short, the solutions to the problems described in this essay are:

1. We, as individuals and as a Nation, need to turn to God for His love, His guidance, and His grace. Then we need to:
2. use that love and grace to understand, try to empathize with, and forgive those around us, the same way we all forgive ourselves.
3. Then we all need to follow the CDC guidelines and get vaccinated to help keep ourselves from getting badly sick from the virus;
4. and finally, we all need to wear a mask when around others or in a closed area to help keep from passing the virus to our "neighbor."

ABOUT THE AUTHOR

B RIAN L. MURPHY'S FIRST degree was in business management, which led to an eighteen-year career as an individual contributor, then as a supervisor, and then as a manager in the heart of Silicon Valley. Now, as a teacher for twenty years, he has experienced the educational process from the inside, including being a mentor teacher for a dozen student teachers. Having loved being a teacher, he exposes the problems of the day.

The education industry is in trouble, even dying, and something needs to be done to repair the damage before it's too late. This book is meant to identify and take responsibility for what is going wrong so we can remedy the problems.